Exploring a Sense of Place

How to create your own local program for reconnecting with Nature

Karen Harwell
and Joanna Reynolds

ISBN 0-9786851-0-5

Printed on recycled paper using soy-based inks.

Cover photo: © QT Luong/terragalleria.com

Acknowledgments

The authors gratefully acknowledge the generous support of The Foundation for Global Community, out of which our program and this book grew. We also thank the trustees of this organization for their continuing encouragement as Exploring a Sense of Place became a part of the new organization, Conexions. We are deeply grateful for Thomas Berry, Miriam MacGillis and Brian Swimme, whose work has opened us to the largest context in which to explore the particulars of our place. We acknowledge Derek Harwell, who created a prototype of a Sense of Place about 15 years ago with a seven-week program that served as the inspiration for ours. Derek remains one of our valuable guides today. We acknowledge the original team who researched and shaped the first year of the exploration program with us: Melanie Chandler, David Coale, Liz Holdship, Laura McVittie, Terra Morowitz, Pete Shoemaker, Susan Stansbury, Charlie Tierney and Bob Batchelor, education director of The Foundation for Global Community. Other team members through the years with valuable contributions are Gail Claspell, Valerie Fisher, Steve Hays, Lu Isaacs, Leslie Peterson, Marina Rose and, more recently, Jill Baxter, Julie Good, Maria Grandinette, Jana Tuchman, Gloria Geller, Romie Georgia, Bryce Perry and Tom Cronin, who continue to inspire us with their dedication. We couldn't have done the program without all the gifted guides who have taught us so much, including Elizabeth Andrews, Deborah Bartens, Patricia Becker, Meg Beeler, Kerry Brady, Jesse Cool, Drew Harwell, Walt Hays, Paul Heiple, Jim Johnson, Joe Jordan, Brian Knittel, Leo Laporte, Alan Launer, Targe Lindsay, Tom Lindsay, Joanne Masters, Franklin Olmstead, Katie Pilat and Bonnie Zimmerman. We thank you all.

We acknowledge the Northwest Earth Institute's programs, especially Deep Ecology, which stimulated us to want to get to understand and explore our own bioregion. We also appreciate the invaluable guidance of advisors as we struggled to give form to this book: Peter Drekmeier, Allysyn Kiplinger, Pat Sundermeyer, Anne Thomas, Sue Lyttle, Jim Burch, Richard Rathbun, Debbie Mytels, Kay Hays and Susan Mokelke. Other helpful insights came from Cindy Spring and Sandra Lewis, who founded the East Bay Sense of Place program called Close to Home, and from Jeannie Martin of the Blue Ridge Naturalist's Sense of Place program in North Carolina. In addition, we thank Wileta Burch for allowing us to include her painting of the Palo Alto baylands and Malcolm Margolin, whose book *The Ohlone Way* has been an inspirational resource. We greatly appreciate the generous support of Susan and John Maus, Nancy Schaub and Ann and Hans Zulliger. And finally, we will be eternally grateful to our editor, Ariel Rubissow Okamoto, and designer, Darren Campeau, who brought the book together and made it real.

We appreciate the contributions of all these people, and of all those who have participated in our programs and given us feedback and encouragement, as well as others we might not have named, but who have supported us in our work in one way or another. We are grateful.

CONTENTS

Preface

During the twentieth century, the human community under the leadership of American political, scientific and economic communities created a system of exploitation of Earth for human benefit that has severely damaged the life-giving capacities of the planet. The illusion of endless benefits to be achieved has finally collapsed. Yet a remedial program has not yet taken over guidance into the future.

Obviously we cannot create a sustainable future if we do not understand what has gone wrong in the past. Yet the time has come when the negative description of our errors must give way to the surge of creativity that must be the distinguishing aspect of the twenty-first century. This creativity must find expression in four basic fields that largely control the fundamental design of the human venture: the political-social, the economic-industrial, the educational-scientific and the religious-moral. These are the centers of public authority.

Yet these institutions themselves depend on a new awakening of the human intellect, emotions and imagination to a deep inner intimacy with the natural world. We need to experience the dawn and the sunset. We need to feel the cool wind blowing over Earth after a warm, sunny day. We need to hear the song of the mockingbird singing from the top of a nearby tree.

We may think that we are beyond all this, that our rational modes of thinking are sufficient, that we can do without such immersion in the world of wonder, beauty and physical excitement, experiences proper to the uncivilized peoples of the past. We may even think of our children as sufficiently fulfilled with television trivia. Yet we are finally learning that these fundamental experiences of the natural world are inherent necessities for us to reason clearly and shape a fulfilling course of human affairs in all their various contexts. Our children especially need these experiences. Yet only if found with their elders can children's early experiences be complete.

How to recover this elementary contact with the natural world is the subject Karen Harwell and Joanna Reynolds have written about in their book *Exploring a Sense of Place: How to Create Your Own Local Program for Reconnecting with Nature.* They have gone beyond simply showing our need for such experiences. Others have taken up this aspect of our new world of the twenty-first century. Fortunately, Karen and Joanna have the genius to show just how small local groups can be organized, how plans can be developed that will bring people out of their confinement into surrounding fields and forests, out into nearby mountains and streams where natural phenomena can be experienced in their true reality.

Exploring a Sense of Place is a unique guidebook with detailed information on how to organize such programs. It is indeed our guide in the twenty-first century.

THOMAS BERRY
JUNE 2006

Orientation

Magic

We saw a bobcat on our very first trip, at Vasco Caves, which has been, and remains, a sacred and powerful spot for native people. Our guide told us about how the territories of three distinct language groups — Ohlone, Bay Miwok and Northern Valley Yokut — converged there, and how pictographs give us a glimpse of the use of this sacred place by spiritual leaders. In the beginning, I was a little skeptical about some of the spiritual aspects of the program — how having a sense of place can lead you to commune with the environment. My initial attitude was, I'm just here for the information. But in the end I had to agree with them: magic happens when 12 of you every month go on a trip and have these incredible guides along. That's part of why I liked the program so much.

LINE MIKKELSEN
CLOSE TO HOME
OAKLAND

Beginning

You don't need to be an expert on your bioregion to launch a Sense of Place program where you live. You just need curiosity and a willingness to connect with your own home. Whether you live in an adobe, skyscraper or ranchette, by the sea, desert or mountains, anyone with an interest in digging deeper into the spirit and nature of the place where they live can start a program. All you need to do is find the storytellers who know and love your bioregion; discover the heroes who have preserved and restored its natural places; and gather up a foundation of ideas, volunteers and materials to help you begin a serious exploration of your backyard. You'll soon find you don't need to visit a faraway national park or tropical rainforest to experience "wilderness" or "nature."

To help you get started, we offer this guidebook. It summarizes how we, a group of like-minded individuals from a place like yours, created the first Exploring a Sense of Place program in Palo Alto, California, in the year 2001. Inspired by Wendell Berry's observation that "you can't know who you are until you know where you are," and by the growing disconnect between our human culture and the natural world it overlies, we created a yearlong program of exploration that has now lasted five years, enlightened 150 people in our community and inspired three other groups to start similar programs — one in Chesapeake Bay, one in the Blue Ridge Mountains of North Carolina and another here in the San Francisco Bay Area.

Western Labrador-tea, *Ledum glandulosum*

This program is designed to help you come home to your place in the natural world. While most of us recognize where we live by the cities, buildings, supermarkets or sports teams around us, far fewer of us identify with and understand the natural ecosystem that supports us, and of which we are a part. You may be new to a place or have lived there all your life, but there is probably much to discover within a few miles of home.

The Exploring a Sense of Place program provides a series of readings, walks and encounters designed to build a "rootedness in place" and to reconnect our spirits and souls to nature. It seeks to help us establish new patterns in our lives, and experience a shift in our perception. Through regular immersion in nature over a period of time, and guided by the stories and experience of dedicated naturalists and elders, we find ourselves opening up to the true nature of the place where we live and experiencing increased respect and awareness of kinship. As we all gain a "sense of place," we begin a deeper relationship with place, planet and each other.

In more practical terms, we've designed our program as a course of enrichment evenings and Saturday explorations (visits to forests, overlooks, creeks, farms and other key features of the natural world in our backyard). Every month we focus on a different theme — from geology and climate to wildlife and stories of the indigenous peoples — and conclude the year together with a homecoming emphasizing restoration and preservation. Though on the surface it may seem like we're learning about rocks or flowers or birds, the ultimate result is much deeper — an experience of place. By using different lenses, we develop skill in using all of our senses. And by experiencing this together, we form community with those around us.

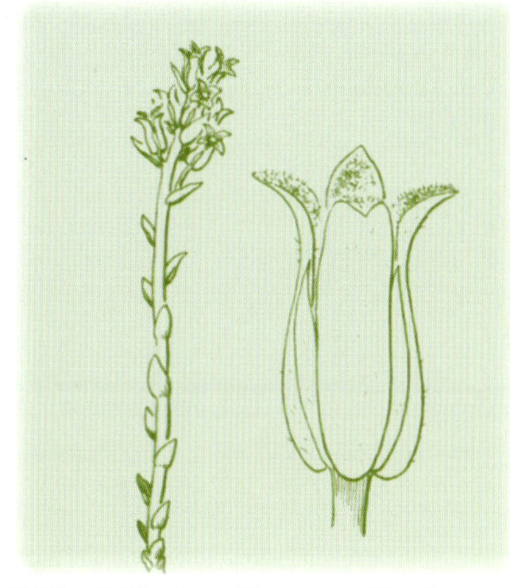

California Pinefoot, *Pityopus californicus*

Now you may be thinking about creating your own new connection to place. This guidebook should provide inspiration, as well as practical information on how to start this kind

You can't know who you are until you know where you are.

WENDELL BERRY

> To see a World in a Grain of Sand
> and Heaven in a Wild Flower
> Hold Infinity in the palm of your hand
> and Eternity in an hour.
>
> **WILLIAM BLAKE**

of program in your own region. It tells you how to get started, how to identify areas of focus and how to find the best people to guide and inform your activities. It also includes step-by-step planning guidance, as well as sample exercises, schedules, forms, flyers and other materials.

Using this guidebook as a workbook, you should be able to customize your program to your own bioregion or watershed. As your program takes shape, you may find you are following our guidebook or have found another pathway that works better for you. Whether you put on a full-fledged yearlong course as we have done, or a more limited experiment, we invite you to keep in touch with our Palo Alto, California, team. We want to learn from your experiences and be able to share them with others.

Let your adventure begin...

The Meaning of Sense of Place

If "you can't know who you are until you know where you are," as author Wendell Berry wrote, then exploring a sense of place should help us discover a sense of self. At The Foundation for Global Community in California, which launched the Exploring a Sense of Place program in 2001, we have always embraced the idea that we all belong to a universe that is one — an interdependent whole. Because the universe is so vast, it is hard to grasp the relevance of this concept of interconnection in our daily lives. So we decided to create a program that would ground the abstract idea of our universal connection to a specific place and time — our local bioregion. We see this program as a doorway to the greater whole. Another doorway comes to us through computers, satellite photography and the Internet. In this amazing time we live in, we are suddenly able to see and experience the world as one Earth. And as a result of our ability to communicate globally, we have the potential to benefit from the feedback of the planet — to experience the hurricanes, earthquakes and tsunamis — whether or not they are occurring in the area where we live. It's as if the planet is inviting us to open ourselves to the powers of nature.

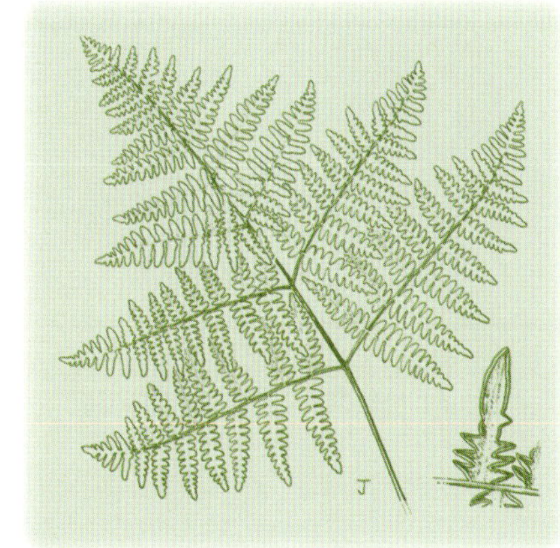

Brake, *Pteridium aquilinum*

Loss of Sense of Place

We've all heard people say they "love nature." Yet we often forget what great skill humanity has in constructing a world that insulates us from actually having to experience nature. Our days are lived mostly within a world of cars, houses, offices and malls, all heated or cooled to comfortable year-round temperatures, decorated with exotic plants and supplied with goods and foods available year-round from all over the world. In this context, we could be living anywhere. The Western world, from the perspective of the steering wheel, keyboard, television remote or cash register, looks pretty much the same

Cascara, *Rhamnus Purshiana*

I do not know whether it is possible to love the planet or not, but I do know that it is possible to love the places we can see, touch, smell and experience.

DAVID ORR
EARTH IN MIND

wherever we go.

Though this world does supply us with a great deal of comfort and convenience, many of us feel there is a cost to our insulation: a sense of loss or dissatisfaction. After building on and paving over the land, damming up and rerouting waterways, planting parks and gardens, we have erased the surface of nature around us, as well as crowded out other species. In so doing, we have created our own artificial human-based bubble of habitat. While in the days of the first Native Americans this habitat might have been based on natural rhythms and resources, over the years we have grown farther and farther from the influence of nature. Building and living free from nature's ways and whims is our new way of life.

BioQuiz:

How many days until the moon is full ?

Many of us believe that if we are to be a successful species in the long run, we need to burst our bubble, change our ways and partner with nature. We believe that Exploring a Sense of Place can be an effective way to begin bursting the bubble. Then we can start the process of becoming native to this place.

Fortunately, others have started before us in other ways. Many visionaries in our culture have loved, preserved and defended natural places threatened by development and other encroachment, and have worked to set aside land as wilderness, parks and open space. We are indebted to them and can learn from what they passed on to us, and find ways ourselves to foster a healthier world for our children and the children of all species.

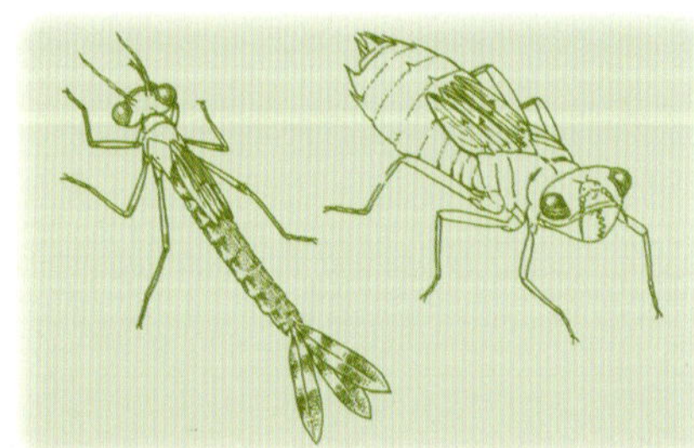

Dragonfly Larva

The San Francisquito Program in a Nutshell

In this section, you will find a brief review of some of the ideas and concepts that led to our creation of the Exploring a Sense of Place program in California. In the chapters that follow, you will find more detail on exactly what steps we took to develop, organize and carry out the program, and lessons learned in the years since its inception.

Determine your place

First, wherever you live, you need to determine the focus of your exploration — your *place*. As you define your place, try to see beyond city and county boundaries to the underlying larger landscape and ecology. Beginning the design process for our program, for example, we recognized that we live in one of the most diverse bioregions on Earth. Here on the San Francisco Bay peninsula, within a 50-mile radius, one can move from an ocean ecosystem to a redwood forest, down through an oak savannah and out onto the wetlands and the bay estuary. Having that much diversity in such a limited geographic area is very unusual, so we decided to concentrate our attention specifically on our own watershed within the larger bioregion.

Mesquite, *Prosopis juliflora*

Out of this large and diverse region, our California team designated the San Francisquito Creek watershed as our *place*. But you may define your place in an entirely different way. For some ideas about how to think about bioregions, see p. 16.

Find the stories of your place

Though they differ in specifics, every place is made up of the same archetypal stories. Seek out these stories and you have the framework to design your own Exploring a Sense of Place program. Though what you first see may be the superficial story of human construction (cities, roads, institutions), look for the underlying story of the place to really get to know it. For instance, the result of the geologic story of the area's formation over time is seen in its current features — mountains, lakes, desert terrain or marshland. What is this deep-time story?

Every place has a story of its earliest people and how they were sustained and influenced for thousands of years. It has its weather and climate — the patterns of temperature, humidity, water- and airflow, and so on. And, of course, all of these stories and patterns are interrelated. For example,

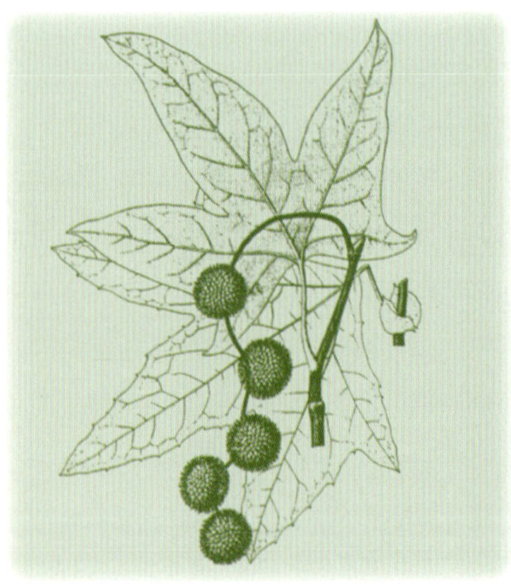

Western Sycamore, *Platanus racemosa*

the weather, geology and types of plants that thrive determine the kinds of animals that will inhabit the place. Over eons, these living communities have worked out how to live together sustainably, adapting to seasonal and environmental change. We need to know these stories, and to tune into how these communities are adapting to the stresses brought about by the rapid changes of human development. If we pay attention, these stories will lead us deeper into a sense of place (see also p. 20).

Create a new pattern in your life, for all seasons

To begin to appreciate the wonder of the natural ecosystem that supports our living here, it is necessary to create regular encounters and experiences in nature. So whether your course of exploration is one month or one year long, or something in between, the necessary ingredient is the establishment of a regular pattern in your life. Sometimes it may seem easier to stay in and be comfortable, especially in "bad" weather. But we have found that experiencing our home in all weather and all seasons can be full of wonderful surprises, such as how green and lush and budding with the promise of new growth the forest is in the wetness of winter. Whether it's raining or windy, cold or hot, every month we go out, establishing a regular pattern of listening, noticing and learning from nature's wisdom.

Find good guides, and listen to them

If you begin asking around, you will find many wonderful storytellers, elders and naturalists whose knowledge can guide your growing sense of place. In our program, we have different guides each month. They are passionate about their expertise and happy to share their insights. As a start, you might check with your regional parks and environmental education groups for naturalists and guides. It helps to explain the purpose of your program, and what you are looking for in a guide. You want someone who can help your participants connect with the story of the place, not just produce a lot of information. Always ask for recommendations. One good guide often leads to another.

Design your program for a sense of wholeness

You will design your program according to your own bioregion, and it may look very different from ours. In the planning process be sure to keep in mind the whole program and how each exploration relates to the others. A goal of our program is for participants to develop an appreciation for our watershed as a whole — rather than experiencing the course as a series of unrelated outings. The following sequential outline of our program is intended to serve as a brief illustration, to show how all the parts create an integrated, yearlong experience (a more in-depth outline appears on p. 45):

Coast Live Oak, *Quercus agrifolia*

So that we can begin with an overview of the region that encompasses the course, our exploration together starts on the fourth Saturday in May on a ridge at the highest point of our watershed. From here we can see the whole terrain we will be exploring over the course of the year, all the way out to San Francisco Bay, and observe how weather patterns arising from the Pacific Ocean sweep over the land and create the unique climate of our region.

In June, the program proceeds down the watershed through the redwoods to the oak savannah. Each month, it includes something about the ways of the Ohlone people, the Native Americans who have lived here for more than four thousand years. So during our time in the oak savannah, for instance, we learn how the acorn was integral to the life of the Ohlone, and that their calendar was based on the oaks and the availability of acorns.

In July, when portions of San Francisquito Creek (the watershed's primary stream) are dry, our midsummer exploration takes us down into the creek bed where, as we walk, we experience the uniqueness of a riparian ecosystem. This is our opportunity to become acquainted with the varied plant life here and, when finding signs of animals, to learn that many creatures, including mountain lions and coyotes, use the creek as a corridor.

Coyote, *Canus latrans* (top) and Gray Wolf *Canus lupus* (bottom)

In August, the view expands and focuses on our place in the cosmos. This month's exploration begins in the early evening with a walk to the top of a nearby mountain. After experiencing the sunset and moonrise — opening our imagination to realize we are on a revolving planet within a revolving solar system within a revolving galaxy — we return quietly back down the path through the hills, guided only by the light of the stars and moon.

At harvest time in September, the focus is on nourishment. At a local nature preserve and organic community farm, we learn about wild edibles and how the Ohlone nourished themselves while living in our watershed, as well as ways we could be sustaining ourselves today. We experience the bounty of the land, fresh and wholesome, and free of artificial fertilizers and pesticides.

Killdeer, *Charadrius vociferus*

In October, our exploration takes us out to the baylands at the place where the San Francisquito Creek flows into the San Francisco Bay estuary. Here the water, having fallen as rain and coursed through our watershed, returns to the bay and then out into the Pacific Ocean, available to start its journey over again as it evaporates into clouds. Our guides introduce us to the wonders of the estuary — from tides to all the many shorebirds and saltwater plants.

Our November exploration is a return to higher elevations to revel in the beauty and lushness of the upper watershed as we explore the tributaries that come together as San Francisquito Creek. As a special feature of this day, a couple of hours are set aside after lunch to go out individually on our own nature quests, coming back together for the last hour for a rich sharing with one another.

In December, we honor winter as the time of creativity in ourselves as well as in nature. Going out into the winter forest (no matter what the weather) is a unique opportunity to open all our senses and experience the textures and vibrant colors of the mosses, lichens and mushrooms. In celebration of the creativity in all, this

Elements of Exploration

- **Approach with an attitude of respect and humility — a not-knowing.**
- **Expose yourself to nature. Go out into your bioregion and experience it directly. Don't just read about it, look at pictures of it or think about it!**
- **Establish a pattern of spending time in and observing nature.**
- **Be open. Free yourself from blocks. Allow yourself to be imprinted by nature.**
- **Pay attention. Be present. Focus on different aspects of nature each time.**
- **Explore with all of your senses: experiment with sound, touch, smell, taste and sight.**
- **Follow your feelings: curiosity, awe, gratitude.**
- **Explore your wonder: ask questions, engage.**
- **Notice the language you use to describe place. Try to move away from the language of things and objects and into the language of reverence.**
- **Learn in community. Find the people who are familiar with the place to guide you. Explore with a group of people, sharing your insights with others.**
- **Respond. Express yourself in poetry, music, art, dance or however you feel moved as you engage with nature.**
- **Find ways to design your life and our community life with nature in mind.**
- **Celebrate belonging!**

day includes the creation, by each of us, of an earth sculpture (taking the idea from the work of Andy Goldsworthy). Photographs of each of these creations become a slide presentation opening our next evening orientation.

In January, when the ground is wet from the rains, our guide in exploring a local preserve is a tracker, who awakens us to all the signs of elusive wildlife in the area. We learn to discern evidence of animals' presence and activity from tracks, scat, rubbings on trees, burrows, trails they follow and nests they build.

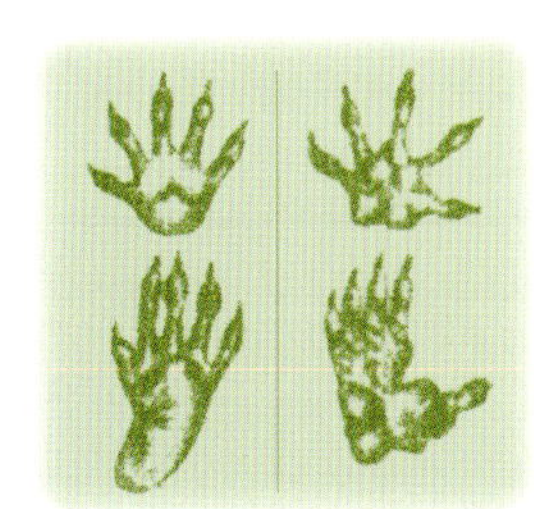

Hand and foot tracks of Raccoon (left), *Procyon lotor* **and Opossum (right),** *Didelphis*

Because we recognize the importance of seeing how our place changes with the seasons, the course is designed so that we return to some of the ecosystems more than once. So in February, our exploration returns to the baylands, this time to experience the migrations of the ducks, geese and shorebirds.

And in March, we return to the oak savannah to witness the flowering of the oaks and the extravagance of the spring wildflowers, as well as to focus on human efforts toward preservation and restoration of native plants.

BioQuiz:

When do deer rut in your region?

For our final exploration, in April, we return to where we began at the top of the ridge — only this time, arriving before the sun has risen. Together we have the joy of greeting the day looking out over our watershed and, after all we have learned, having the experience of returning home, and as T. S. Eliot so beautifully put it, "knowing the place for the first time."

By designing the course in this way, our hope is that by the end of the year's exploration, participants will recognize the integration of all aspects of our watershed as one living system. In this way, we all awaken to what a watershed is and realize how nourished we are by the place that sustains us.

Find references

As you are planning for your Exploring a Sense of Place program, you will want to immerse yourself in some of the many wonderful and inspiring books about nature. In our Resources section, we include books on bioregionalism, ecoliteracy, deep ecology, cosmology, trees, birds, geology, meteorology and more. There are also some good Web sites you might visit to get you started. We recommend these resources to enhance your program, but they are only supplemental. They cannot substitute for a sustained, direct relationship of your own in your bioregion.

Bioregion As Place
Five Perspectives

We all live on one planet, and yet, the beauty and strength of this Earth does not derive from a single global sameness, rather from articulation in arctic and tropics, seacoast and mountains, plains and valleys, deserts and woodlands. Everywhere on Earth, life is established on a functional community basis. Each distinctive bioregion is composed of mutually supporting life systems that have organized and sustained it over vast expanses of time…

A bioregion is an identifiable geographical area of interacting life-systems that is relatively self-sustaining in the ever-renewing processes of nature. The full diversity of life functions is carried out, not as individuals or as species, or even as organic beings, but as a community that includes the physical as well as the organic components of the region.

– THOMAS BERRY, *THE GREAT WORK*

Bioregionalism is an age-old way of viewing the world. Regions are not delineated by imaginary, straight lines as scribed by humans, but by the climate and land forms which make that part of the planet uniquely distinct. Local life forms, cultures, traditions and hopes for the future reflect that particular place on the planet in which they're rooted.

– RON HUGHES

To become "dwellers in the land," to regain the spirit of the indigenous people, to fully and honestly come to know the earth, the crucial and perhaps only and all encompassing task is to understand the place, the immediate, specific place, where we live. . . .We must somehow live as close to it as possible, be in touch with its particular soils, its waters, its winds. We must learn its ways, its capacities, its limits. We must make its rhythms our patterns, its laws our guide, its fruits our bounty.

That, in essence, is bioregionalism. A bioregion is part of the earth's surface whose rough boundaries are determined by natural rather than human dictates, distinguishable from other areas by attributes of flora, fauna, water, climate, soils, and land forms, and the human settlements and cultures those attributes have given rise to.

– KIRKPATRICK SALES

I do not know whether it is possible to love the planet or not, but I do know that it is possible to love the places we can see, touch, smell and experience. And I believe, along with Simone Weil, that rootedness in a place is "the most important and least recognized need of the human soul.".... The second decision that we must make, then, has to do with the will to rediscover and reinhabit our places and regions, finding in them sources of food, livelihood, energy, healing recreation and celebration.

Whether one calls it "bioregionalism" or "becoming native to our places" it means deciding to relearn the arts that Jacquetta Hawkes once described as "a patient and increasingly skillful love-making that [persuades] the land to flourish."

California Blackberry, *Rubus ursinus*

It means rebuilding family farms, rural villages, towns, communities, and urban neighborhoods.

It means restoring local culture and our ties to local places.... It means reweaving the local ecology into the fabric of the economy and life patterns while diminishing use of the automobile and our ties to commercial culture. It means rediscovering and restoring the natural history of our places. And, as Gary Snyder wrote, it means finding our place and digging in.

– DAVID ORR, *THE EARTH IN MIND*

Bioregionalism recognizes, nurtures, sustains and celebrates our local connections with: land; plants and animals; rivers, lakes and oceans; air; families, friends and neighbors; community; native traditions; and systems of production and trade.

It is taking the time to learn the possibilities of place. It is a mindfulness of local environment, history and community aspirations that can lead to a future of safe and sustainable life. It is reliance on well-understood and widely used sources of food, power and waste disposal. It is secure employment based on supplying a rich diversity of services within the community and prudent surpluses to other regions.

Bioregionalism is working to satisfy basic needs through local control in schools, health centers, and governments. The bioregional movement seeks to re-create a widely-shared sense of regional identity founded upon a renewed critical awareness of and respect for the integrity of our natural ecological communities....

Bioregionalism begins by acting responsibly at home.

– WELCOME HOME STATEMENT,
NORTH AMERICAN BIOREGIONAL CONGRESS
1984

Monterey Pine, *Pinus radiata*

Take it from here

You are now ready to develop your own program in your bioregion. We encourage you in your own creativity as you design and build your program, and we are here to help. In the Organization chapter beginning on p. 25, you will be guided through a step-by-step process — from gathering your team to launching your program. This process is based on our more than five years of experience, and includes schedules, examples, exercises and references.

Barberry, *Mahonia*

Conversations

The kinds of conversations you have outside are somehow different than the ones you have inside. When you're outside, a feeling settles in; the place is working on the conversation. There are many ways you're affected by place. It's a two-way street — it's not just our impact on nature, it's nature's impact on us.

I particularly loved our creative day, when I looked through a loupe at a piece of lichen. We did some contour drawings as a first way to really look. And then, still looking through the loupe, we were asked to find words to describe it, to complete the sentence "this reminds me of" or "this makes me think of." We came up with a huge list of words and then drew upon them to write a poem.

A sense of community begins to happen among people. If we are going out to the oak chaparral, on the Monday evening before that, one of the team members will ask something like, "Is there a tree that was particularly meaningful to you in your life, and would you like to share that with us?" I grew up in New York, and when I first started doing this, I thought, this is such a California thing, maybe I can come to class a half hour later. But I found myself caught up in the shared stories, which became little touchstones; it's very tender in a way.

MARIA GRANDINETTE
SENSE OF PLACE
PALO ALTO

Foundation

Every Place Has Its Story

In order to know the bioregion in which you live, you need to learn its unique story. Though bioregions differ in specifics, every place is made up of stories in common with every other place. Every place has its deep-time geologic story, its earliest people stories, its weather and climate story, its wildlife — plant and animal — stories. If we are only looking at the superficial stories of human construction and resulting artifacts, we may miss the underlying stories of our landscape, ecology and place.

The Deep-time Geologic Story

When you begin your exploration, it is easy to assume the landscape of the region where you live has always been similar to how it is now. Rather, its appearance at any one time represents a fleeting episode in an ongoing story — a story of struggle in which powerful forces from within the Earth are arrayed against forces from without.

Becoming attuned to the ongoing dynamism of the Earth building process — the restless and yet slow-moving currents of circulating hot rock inside the Earth's mantle breaking up our planet's rigid outer rind, a layer termed the *lithosphere*, atop which we live, into huge curved slabs and over time thrusting it into mountains — all of this changes our perspective and evokes a sense of living in the midst of an evolving process.

We may picture this activity as cataclysmic and yet from a human timeline it is painfully slow. The only sudden movements occur with earthquakes, which capture attention, while most of the activity results in only a few inches a year with an infinitesimal slow buckling. However, the cumulative effects of even these imperceptible movements are eventually the lofty mountain ranges of the Earth.

Against the powerful internal forces are the external forces that are less spectacular, operate more subtly and are largely unnoticed. These are the forces of weathering and erosion that slowly but relentlessly erode as the mountain building occurs from within.

By exploring a sense of place we are offering opportunities to expand our awareness in time as well as in space. The deep-time geologic story

Rock

Solid, fluid, slow.
(Mostly space, even so!)
Formed from fire — molten flows,
Shattered, lifted from below
Then carved and worn down, crushed, and though
It seems it's stuck and dead — not moving,
In the long run it's still grooving!
Flowing, slowly, always changing
Over many lifetimes ranging.
Our foundation, inspiration
And a fluid invitation
To participate in life
And in each other without strife.
For as wind and water smooth the rock, and tiny pieces wear away,
They join the flow of love and life as tender leaf or bird of prey.
You and I, and Rock and Crane
Are new and old and back again.
I am strong and I am free
Only when I am me.

JOANNA REYNOLDS
SENSE OF PLACE
PALO ALTO

The Earth is an anomaly; in all the solar system, it is, so far as we know, the only inhabited planet. If we look at the fossil record, we see that after flourishing for 180 million years, the dinosaurs were extinguished. Every last one. There are none left. No species is guaranteed its tenure on this planet. And we've been here for only about a million years, we, the first species that has devised the means for self-destruction. We are rare and precious because we are alive, because we think. We are privileged to live, to influence and control our future. We have an obligation to fight for that life, to struggle not just for ourselves, but for all those creatures who came before us, and to whom we are beholden, and for all those who, if we are wise enough, will come after us.

CARL SAGAN

reveals to us a landscape that is the culmination of a remarkable series of natural sequential events that have occurred over millions of years. The major topographic features of the landscape — the ranges, the valleys and basins, as well as the innumerable smaller features — are the result of ancient events slowly modified over long periods of time. It is through delving into the past that we come to account for and appreciate the present beauty and unfolding story of the place where we live.

The Weather and Climate Story

The weather affects all things on Earth. Over time it has been integral to the deep-time geologic story in its significant role in shaping landscapes. The weather influences the way living beings live, where they live, how they protect and transport themselves and even their moods.

Weather is the conditions that exist in the air around us at any one time: the temperature and pressure of the atmosphere, the amount of moisture it holds and the presence or absence of wind and clouds. The sun fuels the weather. The surface of the Earth is warmed by sunlight — most intensely at the tropics while the poles receive the least. Only half the energy coming from the sun to the Earth is

BioQuiz:

From what direction do winter storms arrive?

absorbed by the Earth's surface. The other half is reflected back into space or absorbed into the atmosphere. Temperatures on land change more than those in the oceans. These temperature differences generate pressure patterns that cause winds to blow, and they also set in motion the vast circulation of the atmosphere, which in turn produces the Earth's weather and climate.

Winds constantly circle the Earth. They bring rain and influence temperatures. The polar easterlies (cold winds blowing from high-pressure regions over the poles), prevailing westerlies (warm, moist winds blowing toward the poles from the subtropics) and trade winds (dry winds blowing from the north- and south-east toward the equator, and replacing rising, warm air) are called prevailing winds because they cover large sections of the Earth. Small, circular wind flows are called cells. Jet streams move air between these cells high in the atmosphere and at very high speeds. Ocean currents follow the direction of the prevailing winds and affect both the climate of the Earth and our daily weather. Since the surface of the Earth is not heated equally, this sets up the circulations of air that produce the Earth's climates. The distribution of land and sea on the Earth, and the presence of mountain ranges, also affect climate.

Following the climate and weather story is one of the most fascinating ways to make connections between Earth's places and ecosystems, and to understand how your bioregion fits into the whole.

The Seasons Story

For most of our history as humans, we have lived more closely connected to nature because we were part of agricultural societies and the seasons continually framed our lives. Our lives were dependent on the cycle of seasons. With the advent of the industrial era, we have developed mechanisms that moderate the sensations of hot and cold and make our dependency seem less relevant.

Most of us are well aware of the rhythmic changes in the weather patterns during the course of a year called seasons. Four seasons — winter, spring, summer and autumn — regularly occur in many areas of the Earth, while in some others there are only two — a wet season and a dry season. As the Earth circles the sun, it tilts at an angle. For six months of the year, the Northern Hemisphere of the Earth tilts toward the sun and experiences long, warm summer days while the Southern Hemisphere has short, cool winter days. During the next six months, the reverse occurs and the Northern Hemisphere tilts away from the sun resulting in winter conditions while the Southern Hemisphere experiences summer.

During the solstice on December 21, the sun appears to stop moving south, giving the Southern Hemisphere its longest day and the Northern Hemisphere its shortest. And then again on June 21, the sun appears to stop moving north, giving the Northern Hemisphere its longest day and the Southern Hemisphere its shortest. During the spring equinox on March 21 and autumn equinox on September 23, the sun is directly over the equator, resulting in day and night being the same length.

The length of the days and seasons, and their dryness and wetness, fluctuate each year. Climate is the typical weather pattern of a region, based on an average of those weather conditions over a period of thirty years or more. Living as we do in a time of global climate change, even slight fluctuations in weather conditions are more noticeable when they differ from the norms of the seasons we are used to experiencing. Connecting the concept of global warming with even slight shifts in the seasons gives the concept relevance in our lives and activates our relationship with the Earth.

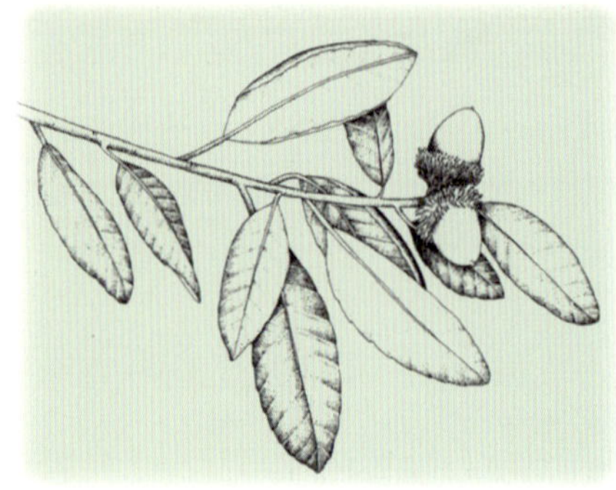

Tanoak, *Lithocarpus densiflorous*

The Story of Indigenous People

Not so long ago in Earth time, the indigenous people of our continent were hunting, fishing and collecting grass seeds on the very land upon which we live. Wherever we are living, the area is vastly different from what it was centuries ago, altered by the colonization and development, the farming, logging, mining, draining and filling of so much of the natural landscape by immigrants from elsewhere in the world. As writer Malcolm Margolin put it in writing about the Ohlone people of the San Francisco Bay region, "Their whole

The Ohlone Way

[The indigenous Ohlone people had] a balanced (rather than exploitive) relationship with the environment; an economic system based on sharing rather than competing: a strong sense of family and community: social moderation and restraint; the opportunity for widespread artistic creativity; a way of governing that serves without oppressing; a deeply spiritual sense of the world. . . . [They provide us with] a vision of how a Stone-Age people, a people we have so long belittled, had in fact sustained a life of great beauty and wisdom. This realization leaves us feeling curiously rich, as if we had just inherited great wealth from a distant relative we scarcely knew. The wealth, of course, is not one of artifacts and treasures — of these the earlier people had few — but rather the richness of knowing that we are all part of a species with extraordinary wisdom and virtues, a species that can adapt to its environment and create for itself a successful and satisfying way of life.

MALCOLM MARGOLIN

way of life is gone and replaced by a civilization technologically more advanced than theirs, but in many respects ecologically, socially, and spiritually more backward."

As you begin uncovering the story of the indigenous people in the bioregion in which you live, you may wish to examine some of your initial assumptions. "I pictured them as a Stone-Age people with a simple, crude culture — a people who went naked, lived in huts, and survived by means of a few appropriate and skillful technologies such as processing acorns, weaving grasses into baskets, and chipping stones into arrowheads," writes Margolin. What he found through his research was a much more complex and subtle culture with a tremendous wisdom about life and the place they lived.

As you begin to explore a sense of place, it is valuable to look for signs of a people capable of living for centuries in a place without destroying themselves and their natural environment.

The Watershed Story

No matter where you are or where you live, you are in a watershed. A watershed is a region of land in which all the water drains into a particular body of water. Imagine precipitation in the form of rain, sleet, hail, mist, fog or snow falling from sky to Earth. With its landing a never-ending cycle continues. From the high ground or upstream area of a watershed, or headwaters, these drops of water start their downhill, downstream journey — tiny rivulets flowing into one another and becoming creeks, streams, rivers, ponds, lakes, marshes, bays and estuaries and eventually seas and oceans.

A watershed includes both water and land and has a unique mixture of habitats from brooks, rivers and lakes to forests, farms and even cities. The survival of all living things is dependent upon the continuous cycling of water and nutrients through ecosystems. All through our story as humans, we have organized our presence in places in relationship to water. More than any other environmental factor, access to water determined where humans settled, farmed and prospered.

The area of land encompassing a watershed could be small or large. The size of a watershed, and the speed and direction of flow of its waterways, is determined by landforms. High ground, such as mountain ranges and hilltops, frequently directs the path and speed of water flowing downhill, as well as forming the boundaries between watersheds. Within each large watershed, there are many smaller watersheds. For example, a small creek flowing into the Ohio River has its own watershed, but is also part of the much larger Mississippi River watershed.

Along the edges of a watershed, the precise location where a single drop of water lands could make a difference in its journey to the sea. Rain falling on the prairie could eventually flow into the Mississippi River and south to the Gulf of Mexico. However, if blown by a breeze from the south, that same drop of rain might land within the watershed boundaries of the Saskatchewan River, and then flow east and north to Hudson Bay and the Arctic Ocean. No wonder resolutions are frequently called watershed decisions.

Medicine Walk

We did a "native practices" medicine walk. It's really taking time and being in nature by yourself with no specific objective, just being open to what's there. I saw a lot more when I did that. A red-shouldered hawk came down very close, a deer, other animals. Normally people go out in the woods because they're going to go hike; it's a vigorous activity, exercise. But that's a very different experience from sitting and doing nothing but just be there.

BILL HACKENBERGER
SENSE OF PLACE
PALO ALTO

The Wildlife Story

Our Earth is made up of three biospheres — water, land and atmosphere — that continuously cycle oxygen, nitrogen and carbon from clouds to land and bodies of water and back again. These cycles provide the conditions for life to thrive.

In the vast reaches of our solar system, our Earth is known as the water planet, as well as the green planet, because of its mantle of blue water and green vegetation as seen from space. Water and plants enable other forms of life to inhabit this place. Since plants evolved first, they can exist without animals, but animals cannot exist without plants.

Plants purify the air; they exchange the carbon dioxide exhaled by animals with oxygen; they convert the energy of sunlight into foods that sustain all animals, and from the soil, draw minerals — nitrogen, potassium, calcium, iron — that are essential for animal health and growth. Plants provide shade from the sun, refuge from predators and protection from weather.

Those plants and animals that are native to our bioregions are important to know, as they are fundamental to the health and stability of the local ecosystem. Finding the story of plants in our bioregions can be easier, because plants grow all around us and are rooted in the ground. Animals can be more elusive. But their story can be found in the signs they leave behind — prints and tracks, scat and droppings, rubbings on trees, trails and entrances to burrows, vegetation lines on trees where deer and other browsers have eaten up to a particular level on a tree or shrub. These signs challenge us to never again be as unaware of the presence of wildlife.

Organization

Designing Your Program

Creating a Sense of Place program is a journey. As you design your program, your curiosity and wonder will urge you on. You will select among the many places you can visit, and choose the experts with whom to consult. One discovery will lead to another, and as you find the elders and naturalists who will guide you in your journey, the way will become clear. The many intertwining paths will lead to greater knowledge and experience, augmented by the stories and insights of your fellow travelers. You may find that the territory is so rich and deep that you will need to limit what you can cover in your one-year course; in doing so you will open the door to further exploration in the years to come. In the meantime, here is what we think you need to know to get started.

Carpetweed, *Mollugo verticillata*

As with all journeys, this one begins with some vital first steps. You are setting out to create a Sense of Place program in your own bioregion, and this chapter will guide you in this beginning phase.

Some of the questions we will address here are:

- What are the common elements in exploring the story of a watershed, such as geology, weather patterns, native plants and animals, seasons and indigenous people?
- How do you identify the guides — the people who know and love the place, can tell its story and help the group relate to it?
- Where are the special places you can go to "read" the story of this particular bioregion?
- Do you have a basis to decide which places you're going to include in your schedule and in which season it would be best to visit them?
- How do you find the reference materials?
- How might you balance the experience so that there is an appropriate mix of sensation, information and inspiration?
- How do you enlist others to work with you as a team or sponsor a program?
- What ideas are there for experiences that help participants connect to one another, as well as to place?

Since no two programs will be exactly the same, think of the following steps as a template. We've included on-the-ground examples based on our experience in the San Francisquito watershed, as well as some variations from other programs that have been

California Meadow Vole, *Microtus californicus*

Woodland Trail

With sensuous curves among
the trees,
naked soft 'neath fallen leaves,
my name you whisper, drawing me.

I know not where you call me to,
yet follow blind, eyes open for a clue,
past coyote bush, madrone, and oak,

Until at bay you stop me cold,
caress my palm with feather-fern,
to softly soothe my searching soul,

and bid me sit to write a spell,
then beckon onward, twisting,
turning,
as I look backward, longing, yearning.

But I can't go back, I know that now,
for there lies only history.
It's your siren's call I'm bound
to follow,

leading to my mystery.

MIKE ABKIN
SENSE OF PLACE
HUDDART PARK

modeled on ours. One program, called Close to Home, is located on the east side of the San Francisco Bay, also in California; another program, called Discovering a Sense of Place, is in the Blue Ridge Mountains of North Carolina.

Western Azalea, *Rhododendron occidentale*

As you begin the process, you will see that there are significant decisions for you to make up front. Just keep in mind that you have a great deal of flexibility in making them. The important thing, as you get into the details of planning and then implementation, is that you keep to the spirit and purpose of what you are creating rather than getting side-tracked by the fascinating details.

The 26 steps that follow may seem like a lot to do! As a summary and simple guide to the steps and timing of putting together a program, we have included a sample planning timeline and checklist in the Information chapter (p. 56).

BioQuiz:

Where is the wilderness in your bioregion?

Mock Azalea, *Menziesia ferruginea*

Step 1. Recruit your leadership team.

The first thing to do is to recruit your leadership team and get everyone on board with a shared vision. A supportive team that embraces the vision and work makes it a pleasure to produce the program. Begin by identifying at least one other person who shares your vision and then, between the two of you, identify others who are interested. Look for specific skills necessary for success. At least one of you, for example, should be good at explaining the purpose and spirit of your program to prospective guides and other contributors. You will also need team members who can organize, facilitate, research and market your program. The size of the team you build will depend on the style and extent of the program you are planning, and the time availability and commitment of team members. Above all, gather people with passion with whom you enjoy creating. Don't forget to reach out to community groups, schools or religious organizations. These are good places to find other people to join you in the endeavor, or to recommend someone to you.

Mule Deer, *Odocoileus hemionus*

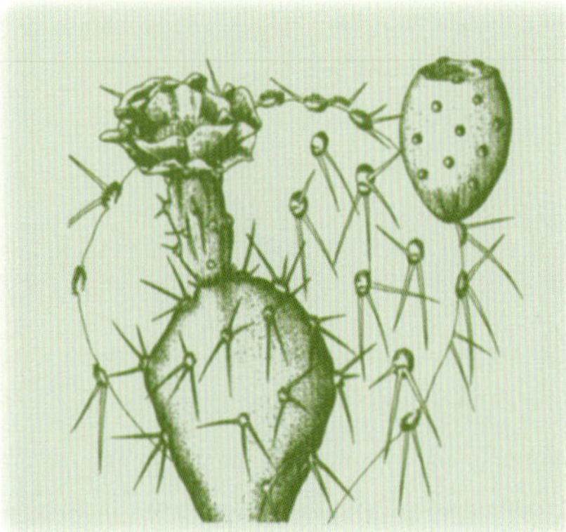

Prickly-Pear, *Opuntia occidentalis*

Once you have your team, be sure to designate a team leader or project director and to orient the rest of the team to your vision. You may wish, for example, to introduce them to the idea of a Sense of Place program by showing them the Sense of Place video (see Resources), as well as this guidebook.

On-the-Ground Example: *The San Francisquito program began only with volunteers (most of whom held full-time jobs) and found that a working group of six to eight was about right. Starting in fall 2001, one person recruited a colleague, and found the rest of the team among participants in a Deep Ecology course we sponsored. The next year's team included some of that original team, augmented by enthusiastic participants from the first year course who were willing to help make the experience available to others. At a very early meeting, we experimented with a few simple exercises to begin to get a feel for what we were aiming at in the program. Some of us began by taking neighborhood walks on a regular basis, along the same route, and noticing subtle seasonal changes. We also spent time in local natural settings, and practiced standing still, closing our eyes and activating all of our senses — noting warmth from the*

Blue-eyed Darner, *Aeshna multicolor*

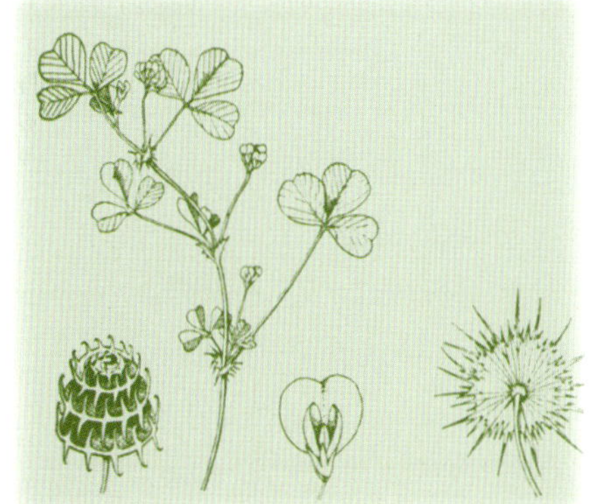

California Burclover, *Medicago polymorpha*

sun, the touch of breezes, the different sounds. It was also interesting to follow a line of questioning like: Why is that bird flying so low? Does it do so searching for food? What else do we notice about its behavior? What does its behavior tell us about its survival strategy?

Step 2.
Recruit sponsors and advisors.

You can establish credibility for your program and gain access to knowledgeable people in your area by recruiting sponsors from local learning institutions. These may be museums, universities or other organizations that focus on the nature and history or preservation and restoration of your bioregion. These organizations would be good places to search for people with expertise whom you can ask to be part of an informal board of advisors. Ideally, your advisors would help you plan the program and find good guides. When these experts hear what you are doing, most will be delighted to assist you in achieving your goals.

Sponsoring organizations can support you in various ways, such as providing community recognition and publicity, networking, naturalist expertise and perhaps even meeting space. Partnering with you can also benefit them. Along with the satisfaction of supporting a valuable new program, they gain networking opportunities and publicity for their own programs.

On-the Ground Example: *The San Francisquito program was developed within an established organization, The Foundation for Global Community, which became its sponsor. As a part of the Foundation we have been fortunate to have office support and meeting space, as well as valuable contacts and advisors both within and without the organization.*

Variations: *The East Bay program was cosponsored by the Oakland Museum,* BayNature *and* Earthlight *magazines, and by the EcoStewards of Montclair Presbyterian Church.* BayNature *played a key role in establishing the program's credibility and in making connections. When the two founders began developing their version of a Sense of Place program in 2003 (calling it "Close to Home"), no one in the world of nature talks and hikes had ever heard of them. So they asked the magazine to invite knowledgeable people who might help them to a brainstorming meeting. Because the magazine saw the fledgling program as noncompeting and complementary to its mission, it agreed to help. And because the magazine lent its name and credibility to the meeting, turnout was good and helped the program get a solid start. Eventually both the magazine and the local museum agreed to cosponsor the program, further increasing its legitimacy. The Blue Ridge program evolved within a university, growing out of a desire on the part of North Carolina Center for Creative Retirement to better introduce Asheville's populace to the mountains, woods and wildlife around them. The 18-year-old center serves a growing community of current and future retirees (boomers). To get them outdoors, the center launched the Blue Ridge Naturalist Program (ongoing in-depth naturalist studies), and the Sense of Place course within it (yearlong course of weekend and evening events). While the latter was created especially to fit the schedules of working people, it has quickly become a*

Tanbark Oak, *Lithocarpus densiflorus*

Western Peony, *Paeonia brownii*

Salt Rush, *Juncus lesueurii*

multigenerational program serving both the employed and retired. Those who've enjoyed Sense of Place have gone on to learn more through the Blue Ridge Naturalist Program.

Step 3.
Decide on the length and structure of your program, and how often it will meet.

Setting a regular pattern, whatever the length or frequency, is a crucial element. You could hold monthly or quarterly explorations for example, or decide on a six-month pilot as a first step toward a longer course. We encourage you to consider a combination of evening indoor orientation events and outdoor follow-up explorations to enrich the experience.

On-the-Ground Example: *The Blue Ridge program learned during its first year that what works for 12 months in California's temperate climate can be too chal-*

California Seablite, *Suaeda californica*

lenging in the extreme winters of North Carolina. Several explorations had to be cancelled due to snow, so the 2006-7 program was cut back to a nine-month period between March and November.

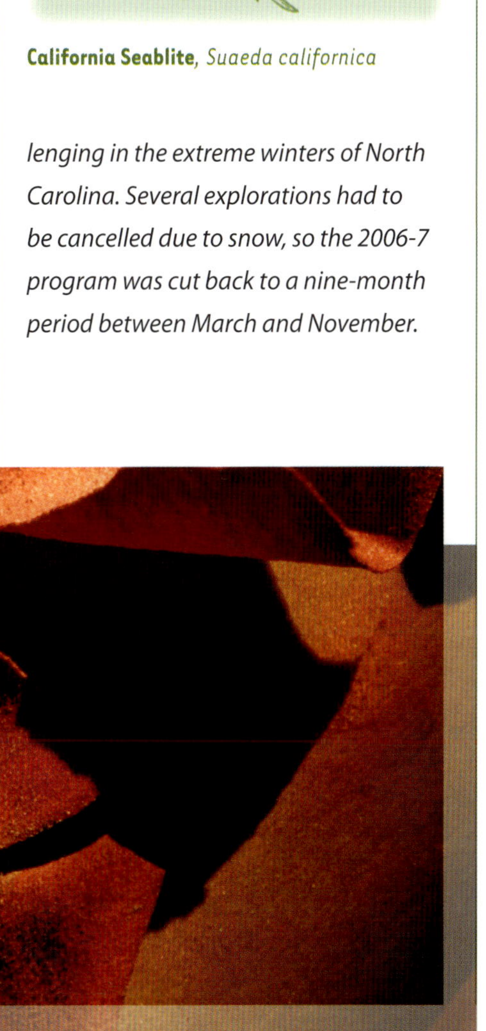

Step 4.
Decide on the size of your program.

The number of participants in your explorations may range from 6 to 30, depending on your goals, skills and outreach for the program. Whether you start with a simple intimate group or strive for a larger, more complex gathering, you'll need to establish a dedicated core of participants. There may also be occasions when you invite a broader public to join you, such as during supplemental evening programs with speakers of general interest (a good way to reach more members of your community and supplement the group's income by charging a small fee).

Step 5.
Set a team meeting schedule.

Decide how often your team leaders will meet during the planning phase, the implementation phase and once the program is launched. It takes time to do research, make contacts and organize the program, so it is important to know who you can count on to carry out these necessary steps.

On-the-Ground Examples: *The San Francisquito course lasts for an entire year, meeting one Saturday a month for the field exploration, and the preceding Monday evening for preparation, enrichment and assimilation. This gives us an opportunity to orient ourselves to that month's location and theme, as well as to assimilate our experiences from the previous month, sharing what we have learned with each other. The evening usually includes a speaker — whenever possible the guide for that month's field exploration. The Monday evening meeting also offers an important opportunity to create community and continuity. Each month we ask participants to introduce themselves to each other in a new way, answering a different question about an early or memorable experience with nature. For example, when the evening's theme was about forests or trees in our area, the question was, "What can you tell us about a special tree in your life, past or present?" Participants also get a chance to reflect together on the previous month's exploration and talk about what moved or surprised them. In the process, they reveal something about themselves and learn more about their fellow travelers. In addition, the evenings allow time to constantly reorient the group. Using a large map of the whole watershed, we take a little time every month to point out where we have been and where we plan to go next. We have found both the evening and day explorations to be not only valuable, but also essential to our program. In terms of the annual schedule, we start and end in the spring so we can appreciate a whole year's seasonal changes and cycles. In determining the number of participants in our course, we set the number at 30, plus team members, as an*

Wood Rat, *Neotoma fuscipes*

Wild Celery, *Apiastrum angustifolium*

outside limit for the exploration days. We felt that more than that would diminish the individual experience, as well as overly impact the area explored. We felt that fewer than 30 wouldn't allow for the inevitable few who would miss a day here and there. Too few people turning up could also diminish the course experience.

Variations: *The East Bay and Blue Ridge programs follow a similar schedule of one weekday evening and one weekend day per month.*

Step 6.
Begin to develop a budget.

Estimate expected costs. This is an important element in your planning, so you can determine how much to charge for the program. If your design is simple and you keep costs down, your program will be more affordable and inclusive. If you include all the "bells and whistles," it could get expensive, and the fee will need to be higher. Alternatively, you could supplement the cost by finding sponsors or donors, or by holding events to raise money. Some budget items to consider where applicable: honoraria or fees for guides and speakers, notebooks and materials, printing and copying, advertising, meeting space rental, insurance and entrance fees.

Striped Skunk, *Mephitis mephitis*

On-the-Ground Examples: *The San Francisquito program covers costs by charging tuition of $375 for the year. (We offer a $50 discount to couples who share one materials binder.) Donations have made it possible to offer some partial scholarships. The largest line-items in our budget are honoraria for guides ($50 to $100 each, depending on expectations, and with multiple guides at times), advertising, materials and copies. We are fortunate to have our own meeting space.*

Variation: *The East Bay program also has been sustainable with the tuition they charge — $375 for the year. One of their sponsors provides meeting space at a low fee. Some of their field trips require special transportation, which is a big budget item, and they typically pay their speakers $100 and guides $250.*

BioQuiz:

{ On what day are the shadows shortest where you live? }

Black Willow, *Salix gooddingii*

Step 7.
Develop a program timeline.

Draw up a timeline of all the tasks that need to be accomplished by the day the program begins. Using a worksheet, such as the sample on p. 56, set up a schedule of what needs to be done when and by whom. Though you will no doubt adjust it as you go along, this will help clarify your process and ensure that everything gets done in a timely manner. You will also want to set up a similar timeline of tasks in preparation for each exploration day.

Step 8.
Do your exploratory research.

Doing the preliminary research for your own unique place is one of the most rewarding aspects of planning. Most of us start with limited knowledge of our place (even if we have lived in it a long time), and the more we immerse ourselves into the research, the more we find ourselves opening doors to discovery we didn't even know were there. Plan on spending a number of months in this stage before you offer the program to the public. Be open and broad in your early research, and leave the shaping and fine-tuning until later, when the emerging territory becomes more distinct. The steps that follow are all part of this research period.

Step 9.
Define your bioregion.

Establish the perimeters of your explorations by defining your bioregion, or the portion of it that can be meaningfully explored in the timeframe of your program. By paying attention to the weather patterns, geology and water flow, you can trace

your own watershed. You may decide to draw the boundaries of your exploration beyond it or within it, but once you have established the parameters, you can explore it as a living system. For some foundational ideas, see Bioregion As Place, p. 16.

On-the-Ground Examples: *For the San Francisquito program, we found that our watershed is a manageable ecosystem to explore within our larger bioregion. The San Francisquito Creek watershed covers an area of 45 square miles (including 13 miles of creeks) and drains from the coastal mountains to San Francisco Bay, passing through both natural and urbanized areas along the way. Several other environmental and citizen stewardship groups working in the same watershed enhanced our*

Blue Oak, *Quercus douglasii*

access to guides, information and like-minded folk.

Variations: *In the East Bay the program has focused on two counties and the public parklands within those counties, and visiting a variety of representational features, with a different emphasis in each year's program. By contrast, the Blue Ridge program explores an ecologically defined bioregion — the Blue Ridge Province of the Southern Appalachians.*

Step 10. Start the search for guides and storytellers.

You may find naturalists at local parks and environmental organizations. At libraries, natural history museums and schools, you can find other guides and start building your lists of contacts and sources, and come up with ideas for good places to visit. Types of people who make good guides include: naturalists, biologists, botanists, geologists and other scientists from the U.S. Geological Survey, local landscape and nature artists, activists from local advocacy groups, and chefs, gardeners and farmers with an interest in sustainable food and agriculture. As you begin to identify these special people and talk with them about the intentions of the program, you will find that not only are they happy to share what they know, they will often refer you to others.

Miner's Lettuce, *Montia perfoliata*

Remember, guides will be responsible not only for introducing your participants to the wonders and secrets of the natural world around you, but also to new dimensions of experience. So you will want to find people who are not only knowledgeable about their subject, but can tell a good story and connect with the participants. Don't just turn yourself over to the experts. Interview them ahead of time; let them know what the program is about and what you want from them. In this way, they will not only act as guides but also contribute more deeply to the goals of your team and program. We have developed wonderful relationships with some outstanding naturalists in our area who return year after year to participate in our program.

Presidio Clarksia, *Clarksia*

Don't forget, some people make their living sharing this knowledge, and some are able to volunteer. Ask about expectations of a fee or honorarium.

**Step 11.
Explore themes
for each session.**

What are the possible themes or emphases you can explore as you visit specific sites in your bioregion? There are many ways you can tell the story of place, and selecting a theme for each day helps organize it. Team members can be assigned to research different ideas and collect available resources. For an introduction to some of the foundational themes of place — geology, weather, indigenous peoples and wildlife — see Every Place Has Its Story, p. 20.

Velvet Ash, *Fraxinus velutina*

Internal bonding with nature and external bonding with the living community of the biosphere influences the quality of all other aspects of our identity and life ... This means discovering the reality of our body-mind-spirit self being deeply, securely rooted in the biosphere. Such groundedness tends to enliven inner feelings of security and strength ... grounded identity has an anchored awareness of organic relatedness with one's body, with the earth, and with the other living creatures that share the biosphere with us. This ecobonding influences, if not determines, how open we are as adults to intimate interaction with nature. Having a solidly grounded identity enables us to become maximally receptive to daily experiences of being nurtured by nature.

HOWARD CLINEBELL
ECOTHERAPY: HEALING OURSELVES, HEALING THE EARTH

**Step 12.
Research the indigenous people.**

You can learn much from the earliest human inhabitants of your bioregion. How did they relate to the place before modern culture established itself? Were they able to sustain themselves? How and for how long? What did they know about the land? Besides books on the subject, you may be able to find people in your area who are cultural archaeologists, or even indigenous descendants who know the stories and ways of these first people and are willing to share them with you.

**Step 13.
Set up a resource file system.**

In order to keep track of the locations, articles, maps, pictures and references you will be accumulating, set up files of contacts, places and themes (such as climate, geology, streams, baylands, native plants and animals). This will serve you well as you finalize your schedule and develop handouts (see Information, p. 61).

BioQuiz:

What are five edible plants in your bioregion?

Step 14. Collect material for deepening experiences.

Start a collection of ideas, articles and exercises that will help people connect in multiple ways with their place by using art, poetry, all of their senses and more. How can these intertwine with themes and places throughout the program, and deepen the experience? See p. 75 for some sample deepening exercises.

On-the-Ground Examples: *The San Francisquito team chose Weather, Watershed and Geology for our first theme and first exploration day. This helps us get an overview and deep-time connection with our place. Some other themes include: The Lower Watershed and the Riparian Environment; Life in an Estuary; Migrations and Reflections; Creativity in Nature; Wildlife Tracking; and Restoration & Preservation. Within every theme, we try to include a story or lesson from our local indigenous culture. Periodically we include deepening experiences ranging from sensory and sharing exercises to meditation and art.*

Here is an example of a deepening experience we organized while hiking over the oak savannah landscape of Edgewood Park. We led our participants through the experience as follows: First, try to tune in to all of your senses. Find a quiet place next to a tree or rock to sit, rest and be still. Next, use your sight to survey the landscape, use your nose to smell the green and brown grasses, use your ears to hear the wind, use your hands to feel the earth. Now focus on a nearby tree and try to answer the following questions: What kind of tree is it? Are you able to identify it after what you learned earlier today? Are there any other creatures living or growing on the tree? How old do you think the tree is? Was it alive when you were born? Was it a seedling when your grandparents were alive? Try to place the tree's growth within your personal history. As a sapling, what kinds of ecological adversity did the tree have to endure? What qualities does the tree possess that have made it successful in this habitat? If you can, get close to the tree so you can really see it, touch it and feel it! What is the tree communicating to you? What are you feeling in the quiet of your soul? Now use your journal or drawing tablet to write or draw whatever is coming through to you. Try to stay present with the tree and with the intention to be with it. Once you return to the group, what can you share about this experience with others?

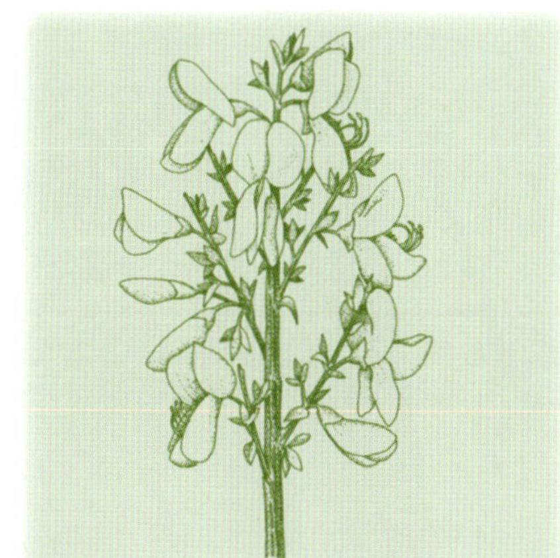

Scotch Broom, *Cytisus scoparius*

> **Live in each season as it passes; breathe the air, drink the drink, taste the fruit and resign yourself to the influences of each. Be blown on by all the winds. Open all your pores and bathe in all the tides of nature, in all her streams and oceans, at all seasons.**
>
> **HENRY DAVID THOREAU**

Step 15.
Select your destinations and set the schedule.

Choose places to visit that illustrate key elements of your bioregion, and can help you understand it as a system. Draw up the schedule for your calendar so that you visit these places in an order that illustrates their connection, and also considers the influence of the season. Weather patterns, water flows, migration routes, Native American trails and many other things can all provide interesting links between places. Your preliminary research will help you define key places to include. In an area rich with resources and many interesting choices, you may find that it can be difficult to narrow down your list of destinations. Consult with your advisors and local experts for their recommendations, but consider what the cumulative effect of your selections will be over the course of your exploration, and how well it tells the bioregional story. We suggest you avoid the temptation to visit only the area's star attractions — those that are most spectacular or obvious. Be sure to include less obvious but perhaps more representational areas too.

A few other things are useful to consider. First, you may wish to choose some places that are visible from each other to enhance the sense of connection. Second, consider planning your program so that you can return to some of the same places but in different seasons. Then you can celebrate and note the change of seasons. Third, we suggest that you select publicly accessible places that people can return to again on their own. These could be nature preserves, parks, designated open space, places of habitat restoration, creeks, rivers or lakes, places of historical interest or any other area that is key to the bioregion in which you live. Once you've selected your

Red Osier, *Cornus sericea*

place list, check to see if you need permits or permission for organized groups to visit. And lastly, before you set your calendar and locations in stone, be sure to line up guides, speakers and experts. Your scheduling may be influenced by their availability.

On-the-Ground Example: *For the San Francisquito program, we made sure to select a few places that were visible from one another. We start our course, for example, in the spring at Windy Hill, on a ridge of the Santa Cruz Mountains. This is a point at the top of our watershed, with a nearly 360-degree view. To the west we see the Pacific Ocean, and laid out before us to the east we can view our whole watershed all the way to San Francisco Bay and beyond. The theme for our first day is Weather Patterns and Geology, which helps us tell our bioregional story in overview. Later on in the year, when we explore the bay's shore, we stand at the mouth of San Francisquito Creek, where it flows into the bay, and look west to see in the distance Windy Hill, where we began. The connection between these top and bottom spots of the watershed becomes almost tangible.*

Wild Mock-orange, *Philadelphus lewisii*

Variation: *The East Bay program selected sites to visit in a different way, largely from established regional parks in the area. Their goals were to select places showcasing all the major natural features of the region, stay within a two-county district and avoid visiting uncomfortably hot places in the eastern county in the summer. Their current program concentrates on the wildlife of the region, and will include visits to their habitats.*

Step 16. Establish a means of communication.

Good communication among team members and program participants is a key to the continued success of the program. It keeps everyone connected and current. Whether the means of communication is on paper or by telephone or email, the important thing is that everyone feels comfortable with it.

On-the-Ground Example: *For the San Francisquito program, we set up two email lists: one for communicating among Planning Team members, used mainly for meeting reminders and agendas, and another list for course participants to remind them of class dates, schedule details, last-minute changes and for sharing other information. Participants also use this vehicle between meetings to share natural happenings occurring in the bioregion, or insights,*

Gorse, *Ulex europaea*

Hop-sage, *Grayia spinosa*

thoughts, pictures or creative endeavors, such as poetry inspired by participation in the course. One person on our team is responsible for managing the email lists.

Step 17.
Decide on the materials and handouts you will use for the program.

Even when you are keeping the program very simple, it is necessary to provide participants with some minimal materials. These include a schedule and description of each day's program, along with any necessary maps or instructions. You may wish to provide some kind of binder to keep all the materials in as the program progresses. If you do so, keep in mind that providing notebooks and materials makes demands on your budget and administrative time.

Choke Cherry, *Prunus virginiana*

On-the-Ground Example: *At the first meeting of the San Francisquito program, we supply each participant with a course binder containing 12 monthly dividers, the year's schedule, a bibliography and a few articles to help orient him/her to Exploring a Sense of Place. Then throughout the year at the enrichment evenings, participants receive a packet of current materials to insert for that month. These include a description of the upcoming exploration day, schedule, maps, directions and lists of what to bring, as well as related informational articles, charts and stories. Participants are encouraged to add their own articles and notes, and thus build a valuable reference resource for the future. For samples of the kinds of things we put in our notebooks, see p. 68.*

Step 18. Set your calendar dates, schedule of places and themes for the entire program.

Once you have done all of your research and made the basic organizational decisions, you are ready to finalize your program based on what you have learned. Be sure to coordinate your calendar dates with other local events to avoid unnecessary conflicts. Give yourself enough lead time before the first meeting to advertise the program and recruit participants.

Black-tailed Jackrabbit, *Lepus californicus*

Step 19. Contact and recruit guides and speakers for each segment of the program.

You may get confirmation only for the first few events, but try to get commitments as early as you can. As we have noted, before confirming your calendar, be sure the guides you want are available for the dates you set. Finalize any financial arrangements with them.

Step 20. Obtain permits or permission (if applicable).

Some public areas require permits if the group is larger than a certain size, if the event is advertised to the public or if money is charged. Before confirming your schedule, contact the entity responsible. If you do venture onto restricted property, you also need special permission.

Bladderpod, *Isomeris arborea*

Step 21. Finalize your budget.

Set program tuition. Base it on the proposed costs, including materials and copies, advertising, honoraria, rental fees, etc., and the proposed number of paying participants. This is when reality sets in. You may have to make some adjustments — if the proposed tuition is too high, you will have to find ways to cut costs or find additional income through fundraisers, sponsors or some other creative means.

Step 22. Set up your administrative process.

Prepare a reliable, clear system for handling the money and registrations. Prepare necessary forms. If you have chosen to set up your program within an existing organization, such as a community group, find out what you need to do to comply with the umbrella group's requirements. If you are not working within an organization, you may have to set up a new entity to handle the financial and administrative side of your program.

On-the-Ground Example: *For the San Francisquito program calendar, we selected the fourth Saturday of every month for the explorations in order to establish an easily remembered pattern. Two exceptions were made: for November and December, we avoid the crush of the holidays by having our exploration on the second Saturday. Our administrative process has been coordinated with the bookkeeping department of The Foundation for Global Community, a 501(c)(3) of which we have been a part.*

Every object, rightly seen, unlocks a new faculty of the soul.

RALPH WALDO EMERSON

Silver Buffaloberry, *Shepherdia argentea*

Variations: *The East Bay program was founded independently, and had to register their name with the county and set up their own bank account (see p. 66 for more details).*

The Blue Ridge program was established under the aegis of the University of North Carolina's non-profit Center for Creative Retirement.

Step 23.
Recruit your participants.

Plan and schedule a free introductory evening a couple of weeks before the first meeting. Invite people to come and learn about your program and give them the opportunity to sign up. Invite friends and associates. Word of mouth works well. So does advertising. You can make flyers and post them at local libraries, stores and meeting places. You can design newspaper ads and articles, get a reporter to write about your program or write a guest editorial for your local newspaper. Place announcements on free community calendars. Write up an enticing invitation to your introductory evening and program and send it out on any appropriate email lists. Those with technical talent on their teams may even wish to create a Web site that includes an up-to-date program description, a registration form, contact information and links to related sites.

On-the-Ground Example: *The San Francisquito program did all of the above, including putting ads in local papers, a couple of weeks in advance of the introductory evening. For samples, see p. 84. To view sample Web sites, go to www.exploringsenseofplace.org and www.close-to-home.org and www.unca.edu/ncccr/brnp.*

Variations: *The East Bay program not only sends out flyers and announcements in search of participants, but also uses them to network with other like-minded individuals and organizations to create a sense of community. To accomplish this, they regularly send outreach materials and email announcements to friends of creeks groups, the local native plant society, the three environmental departments at the University of California, Berkeley, and various community newspapers.*

When the Blue Ridge program first advertised, the course quickly sold out,

And the end of all our exploring
Will be to arrive where we started
And to know the place for the first time.

T. S. ELIOT

Spanish Thistle, *Xanthium spinosum*

forcing the program to start a waiting list. To accommodate a few more, as well as some of the seniors at the retirement center unable to take the hikes, they allowed additional people to come to the lectures. They will not continue this practice in the next course, however, as the lectures became too large and impersonal. But the program continues to build community, creating new partnerships with the nonprofit Southern Appalachia Biodiversity Project, the Western Northern Carolina Nature Center, the Asheville botanical gardens and the local mineral museum, among others.

Step 24. Register participants.

Designate one person to be your registrar and keep track of the participants' contact information and money. Remember to limit the number of participants to your designated program size. If necessary, start a waiting list. Send a confirmation letter to registrants with information about the first meeting date.

Step 25. Prepare materials.

If you are going to give participants a resource notebook, you will need to order supplies (e.g., view binders, dividers, paper), make copies and collate the notebooks before the first session of the program.

Douglas Microseris, *Microseris douglasii*

Step 26. Enjoy and expand your program experience.

Now that you've organized and launched your program, don't forget to keep track of the details and improve on your program as you gain experience. You may also think of ways to expand the reach of your program to other places or other generations. This has been designed primarily for adults, but as the adults get a sense of place, they are more able to pass this appreciation on to others, including their own children or grandchildren. You may want to adapt the program especially for children or teens or families (see hookedonnature.org). Or you may wish to change your program in some other way as time goes by and circumstances and people change. The trick is to remain open and creative, and continue to explore.

On-the-Ground Example: *The Palo Alto program moved forward to carry on its*

work in fresh new ways in 2006, when The Foundation for Global Community closed its doors. For many years, the Foundation, recognizing that natural, social and economic systems are all parts of a single interconnected whole, provided opportunities for people to come together to promote cultural change, facilitate personal development and strengthen community. Though the Foundation closed at the end of June 2006, some of its most potent projects, including Exploring a Sense of Place, have reformed as an independent nonprofit organization called Conexions. The new organization's office remains in Palo Alto.

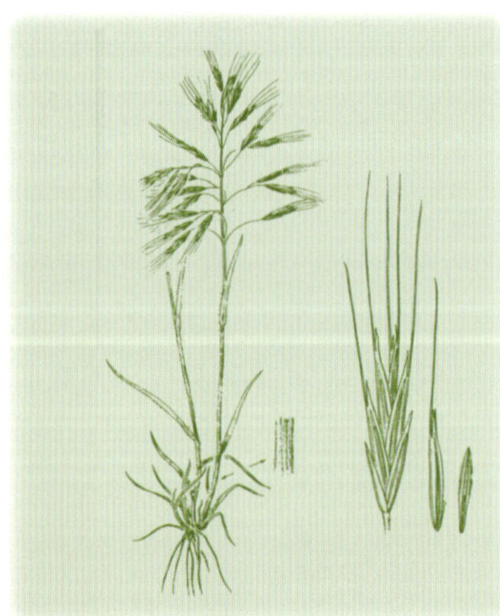

Cheat Grass, *Bromus tectorum*

Variation: *The East Bay program came to a crossroads three years after its inception, when one founder left and the other had to decide whether to repeat the same general ecology focus year after year or to vary the program. Initially, she had thought of running two parallel programs — one with a general ecology focus to bring in new participants every year, and one offering the previous participants a different experience. Unable to do both, the remaining founder decided to let her personal passion for wildlife drive the 2006-7 program. The resulting 12 hikes revolve around seeing the world through the eyes of specific wildlife species. Designing such new perspectives into the course required changing the template and timing of day hikes, and discouraging for the first time photography and socializing along the way. The idea is that wildlife are more likely to show up if they don't sense the dissonance in the woods of visitors chatting and clicking camera shutters, and that undistracted participants will have a greater chance of tuning into the lives of birds, elk, coyotes, salamanders, beetles and other creatures. For a sampling of this year's wildlife hikes, see the 2006-7 Close to Home schedule on p. 82.*

BioQuiz:

{ What are the major natural sounds you are aware of in May ? }

Annual Hairgrass, *Deschampsia danthonioides*

On-the-Ground Example

12-Month Exploring a Sense of Place Program

Palo Alto, California

Orientation: Awakening

Free evening introduction to inspire, inform and enroll participants.

Speakers: Team members explain how the program works, with an emphasis on creating new patterns of relating to the watershed and experiencing all the seasons of our bioregion. We introduce the idea of awakening to what is around us all of the time, but with a new way of experiencing it and a pathway to developing sense of place. We ask participants to visualize their home in relationship to streams, hills, weather patterns, plants and animals rather than to towns or streets. Instead of "I live in Palo Alto," we suggest "I live where the San Francisquito Creek flows down through the redwoods and oak savannah and out into the bay." We discuss how the course will provide a regular opportunity for people to develop their own relationship with the place where they live.

Barrel Cactus, *Echinocactus acanthodes*

Video: View first ten-minute section of Sense of Place video (see p. 91).

Introduction Question: Where is your "bone country"? From what water do you come? (Questions asked in the video by native people describing their relationship with place.)

Deepening Exercise: Using materials provided, draw a map of "home," however you define it. We save these and return them at the end of the year after people have again drawn a map of home and are able to experience how much their perception has changed.

Invite and Enroll Participants: Registration forms are available for participants to sign up.

Weed

On one walk, I focused on a little weed head that had a couple of thorns and some fuzzy stuff. It was a sharp, jerky thing to draw. First we drew with our eyes closed. The guide led us from observation to representation on paper and then to expression in words. I found myself writing some things I was feeling about the culture. Here I was out in nature, and my poem was about war. You could look at this tiny little weed and see a club of war and have something meaningful to say about it. This was not a normal experience for me; it was extra-normal, really moving. It was not so much the surroundings or the people but the careful observation, looking at minute things and opening yourself to a blending of inward and outward experiences. We separate nature and civilization and politics and the environment. My experience showed me that these separations are arbitrary and it's really all of one piece.

ROMOLA GEORGIA
SENSE OF PLACE
PALO ALTO

May - Weather, Watershed & Geology

Exploration Location:
Windy Hill Open Space Preserve

Enrichment Evening: 7 – 9 p.m.

Speaker: Our geologist guide discusses how our watershed was defined by geological formations and weather patterns. We also meet our naturalist guide, who will be leading us on Saturday's meditative walk using all our senses.

Introduction Question: Was there a geological formation — a mountain or range, valley, plains — in your life that made an impression on you when you were young?

Materials: Binder notebooks with orientation materials and May schedule, maps, resources, articles and Ohlone story (local indigenous people).

Field Exploration: 9 a.m. – 3 p.m.

We meet at the top of Windy Hill for a welcome and overview of the day. From there we gain a visual perspective of the entire watershed we call home — standing on the Coast Range with the ecosystem of the Pacific Ocean to the west and the San Francisquito Creek watershed flowing down to the San Francisco Bay estuary to the east. Our guide gives us an historical overview of how geology influences climate, and vice versa, which in turn shapes the landscape and plant and animal communities. Along the way we gain an overview of all the places we will be exploring in our yearlong program, and enjoy glimpses of newts, budding spring flowers and vibrant ferns. Before descending, our guide asks us to shift our sense of sight, using more of our peripheral vision. We come down the hill in a quiet, meditative state, spacing ourselves out, so that we can be more fully present and open to the place. We return to the trailhead to enjoy our lunch. After lunch, we each go off for contemplation time and then return to share insights. We close at 2:30 with a circle of appreciation (as we do at the end of most explorations) before carpooling back down the hill.

June - The Foothills & Oak Savannah

Location: Foothills Park

Enrichment Evening: 7 – 9 p.m.

Speaker: Our speaker is a biologist from Stanford's Center for Conservation Biology. Through his stories and slides we learn about the oak savannah, serpentine soils, native and non-native plants and their ecology within the watershed.

Introduction Question: What is the earliest experience you remember having to do with a tree or trees?

Materials: June schedule and description, maps, resources, articles and Ohlone story.

Field Exploration: 9 a.m. – 3 p.m.

We start this day at Foothill Park. With our docent guide, we then explore the whole ecosystem of an oak savannah — rolling hills, grasses and wildflowers, oak trees, bay trees and chaparral. From a vista point we enjoy a view of last month's location, Windy Hill, and begin to experience the watershed as different areas that each relate to the whole. We ponder such questions as: Why are some hillsides covered with trees while others are covered with chaparral? After lunch, a naturalist guides us in exercises that sharpen our abilities to notice the subtleties of nature. One of the exercises involves each of us making a "sound map." The experiences soon have us laughing at ourselves when, for instance, we discover that we are not able to see things right in front of us! They also help bring the participants together as we chuckle over how little awareness we all have of our surroundings.

July - The Riparian Environment & Watershed

Location: San Francisquito Creek

Enrichment Evening: 7 – 9 p.m.

Speaker: Our speaker is the Stream-keeper of San Francisquito Creek, and has been instrumental in the creek's restoration, preservation and good health.

Introduction Question: Is there a river, creek or stream in your life with which you have had a special relationship?

Materials: June schedule and description, maps, resources, articles and Ohlone story.

Field Exploration: 9 a.m. – 3 p.m.

We focus on San Francisquito Creek and the watershed that encompasses our Place. Originating near the top of Windy Hill, the creek flows through forests, foothills, marshes and out into the estuary. On this day we explore the middle part of the creek with our guide, and learn about one of the last steelhead (a migratory fish) runs in the area. We make our way downstream along the creek to El Palo Alto Park, enjoying several excursions into the creek bed before lunching and hearing stories about the legendary redwood tree, which towered over all of the oaks, and after which the city of Palo Alto is named. After lunch we continue our journey downstream learning more about the ecosystem of the stream — plants and animals and the dynamics of a section of creek that periodically overflows. The experience invites us to shift our perception from one of control over the creek to one of design for living on a floodplain.

August - Cosmology & the Solar System

Location:

Russian Ridge Open Space Preserve

Enrichment Evening: 7 – 9 p.m.

Speakers: We invite two speakers this month, a professor of physics and astronomy who is a scientist with NASA, and a guide who is trained in shamanism and medicine for the Earth. Through the use of slides and illustrations, our astronomer helps us locate our home within the Milky Way galaxy and the universe as a whole. Our other guide, whose work helps people connect more deeply with spirit and the natural world, prepares us for a special Earth Medicine offering on Saturday night.

Introduction Question: What was one of your early memorable experiences with the night sky?

Materials: August schedule and description, maps, resources, articles and Ohlone story.

Field Exploration:

Special time: 5 p.m. – 11 p.m

We begin with a walk to the top of Borel Hill. There we settle on a rocky outcropping, and eat our dinner together, watching the sun set over the ocean. After dinner, we engage in a guided community experience, offering gratitude for the Earth. Following the ritual, we lie on our backs and take in the splendor of the night sky. Our astronomer guide orients us to our Earth as a revolving planet by having us watch the stars on the horizon disappear. He introduces us to particular stars and planets, tells stories of constellations and how they oriented native people, and shares interesting facts about the moon. We share our questions and observations. On the way back down the mountain, we quietly experience the same trail, now in the dark, lit only by the stars.

The Nest

During one Saturday exploration, we were invited to go out in nature and use the materials there to create an ephemeral sculpture. At the time I was hoping to have a child. I found myself making a nest, and realized it was a powerful symbol of preparing for new life. The next year, I missed the Monday night event for that same outing because I was delivering a baby girl.

All my life I've been an urban person. I learn where I am on the grid of sidewalks and freeways, and feel a bit lost if I am away from the grid. Through the course I've come to see how we inhabit and share a watershed. To think of my place, and to see the grid fading and the watershed standing out, has been an amazing shift in perspective for me.

JULIE GOOD
SENSE OF PLACE
PALO ALTO

September - Food: Local, Seasonal & Organic

Location: Hidden Villa Farm

Speaker: Our speaker explores how our choices about the food we eat are important to our sense of place. We discover that the more we choose food that is local, seasonal and organic, the healthier it is for us and for our environment. After a discussion, we view *Beyond Organic*, a video depicting an urban farm that is a model of sustainable food production and community involvement, as well as an inspiration for thousands of people all over the world. (www.fairviewgardens.org)

Introduction Question: Was there a garden in your life?

Materials: September schedule and description, maps, resources, articles and Ohlone story.

Field Exploration: 9 a.m. – 3 p.m.

This day we explore Hidden Villa, a 1,600-acre farm and wilderness preserve. We learn about edible native plants, the farm's Community Supported Agriculture (CSA) program and its gardens and sustainable buildings. To start the day we divide into two groups. One group takes a short walk with a guide to learn about edible native plants and the ways the Ohlone people nourished themselves. The other group meets with a guide to experience the organic gardens. Mid-morning we regroup for a special tour of the sustainable buildings, which use numerous green building practices (straw bale materials, solar electric and hot water, passive solar heating), and were designed to harmonize with the natural surroundings. Then we are led in a food meditation in which everyone places a grape in their mouth and takes a detailed journey as the grape becomes part of us. A local organic restauranteur then provides lunch, and tells us about her use of organic ingredients and foods from local farms that are free of harmful pesticides, preservatives and food coloring. In the afternoon, we reverse our groups and tours, and learn how we can grow some of our food and support local farmers through CSA programs and farmers' markets.

October - Life in an Estuary

Location:
Palo Alto Baylands Nature Preserve

Enrichment Evening: 7 – 9 p.m.

Speaker: Our naturalist uses slides and other tools to give us a preview of the ecological system of the estuary, including shorebirds, fish and even microbes.

Introduction Question: Is there a bay, estuary or marsh experience that you remember?

Materials: October schedule and description, maps, resources, articles and Ohlone story.

Field Exploration: 9 a.m. – 3 p.m.

The Palo Alto Baylands Nature Preserve consists of over 1,600 acres of protected land, including some of the last remaining salt marsh and mudflat habitats on the West Coast. It is also home to some of the last few endangered California clapper rails and salt marsh harvest mice on the planet. We start with an orientation at the interpretive center and examine under microscopes the abundant life in a drop of estuary water. Following that we walk along the bay shoreline and learn about the salt marsh vegetation, shorebirds and waterfowl within view. (In October, many of the ducks are gone, but come February when we return, we will see rafts of these migratory birds.) During the course of the day we see a dramatic tide change. With high tide we look for secretive clapper rails driven up onto higher ground and at low tide we can see avocets and stilts sleuthing for food in the newly exposed mud. During lunch we rest in the shade and discuss the Bioregional Quiz included in our notebooks. It is in a spirit of fun and inquiry that we see how much we have learned in the first six months of our program.

After lunch we explore the place where the San Francisquito Creek flows into the estuary. From this vantage point we can see the expanse of our watershed including all the Sense of Place explorations thus far, noting that the green hills on either side of the creek we visited in May are now brown. And if the tide is low enough, we might be able to see some debris (tree limbs, rocks and the like) that has made that same journey too! To finish our day, we share fresh insights regarding life in the estuary.

November - The Upper Watershed & A Nature Vision Quest

Location: Huddart Park

Enrichment Evening: 7 – 9 p.m.

Speaker: Our naturalist guide prepares us through stories and slides for an adventure in understanding how a watershed comes into being.

Introduction Question: Have you ever had the experience of nature teaching you something?

Materials: November schedule and description, maps, resources, articles and Ohlone story.

Clapper Rail, *Rallus longirostris obsoletus*

Field Exploration: 9 a.m. – 3 p.m.

In the morning, we follow our guide through the upper San Francisquito Creek watershed. We walk along West Union Creek, the uppermost feeder stream, while learning the natural history, plants and animals of the upper watershed. After lunch we meet with a special wilderness guide for an afternoon of deep listening and an individual nature vision quest. As we dwell in the rhythms and cycles of the natural world and deepen into the shifts within us, we awaken to our larger belonging — which is within the Earth community. We quest together as a group and then go off by ourselves for about an hour to develop our ability to listen to the land. Our intention is to apprentice ourselves to the natural world. We gather again for small group sharing of our insights to close the day.

December: Creativity in Nature

Location: Foothills Park

Enrichment Evening: 7 – 9 p.m.

Speaker: Our facilitator is an artist, mediator and psychiatrist, who helps us explore the wonder of creativity in nature. In past years, this exploration has been led by a local artist who paints the hills, waters and skies of our bioregion. She brought examples of her work, and discussed her artistic process and love for the land she paints.

Introduction Question: What is your earliest memory of a connection between art and nature?

Deepening Exercise: While listening to beautiful music, we make leaf rubbings with a variety of native leaves and materials. Beforehand, ask everyone to bring something beautiful from nature.

Materials: December schedule and description, maps, resources, articles and Ohlone story.

Field Exploration: 9 a.m. – 3 p.m.

As we approach the winter solstice, we experience the beauty of winter at Foothills Park, and come to this place with the new perspective of the artist within us. In the morning, we explore our innate creativity by immersing ourselves in nature, with sensory awareness practices, simple meditation, drawing and writing exercises, and experiments with shifting perspectives. We focus on qualities central to cultivating creativity, particularly close observation, interest in process, playfulness, passion and the ability to proceed regardless of expectation and judgment. To help us sit outside for an extended period of time, we have all brought a pad or chair and something warm to drink.

Each of us is also equipped with a large flat piece of cardboard as a hard surface for writing and drawing, as well as some colored pens. After lunch, each person selects a place for creating a design in nature using natural materials from the area. In this design, we attempt to be subtle and non-disruptive. After about an hour, we gather as a group and in silence move around experiencing each person's nature design.

January - Animal Awareness & the Fungus Among Us!

Location: Jasper Ridge Biological Preserve

Enrichment Evening: 7 – 9 p.m.

Speaker: Our animal awareness guide provides an overview and trains us how to detect the presence of animals even though we may not actually be seeing them. Our guide for mushrooms is from the Mycological Society, and amazes us with stories and slides portraying our fungal friends of the forest and the important role these adaptive wintering flowers play in our watershed ecosystem.

Introduction Question: Think of a time when you have been in nature and became aware of the presence of an animal.

Materials: January schedule and description, maps, resources, articles and Ohlone story.

Field Exploration: 9 a.m. – 3 p.m.

At the Jasper Ridge field station, we meet our docents and review the roles each will be providing, so that the focus of the day remains clear. Today's guides include a geologist and specialist in serpentine soil ecology, an Ohlone site guide and two animal awareness guides. We spend the majority of the morning walking and looking for the evidence of animals through their tracks, scat, tree rubbings, trails and nests. During our walk, we also observe mosses, lichens and fungi and their relationship to serpentine soil ecology. On the way back to the station for our picnic lunch, we pass though a riparian forest and witness an abundance of wood rat nests. After lunch, we visit an Ohlone village site and see a grinding stone area and caves where these Native Americans gathered for shelter and ritual.

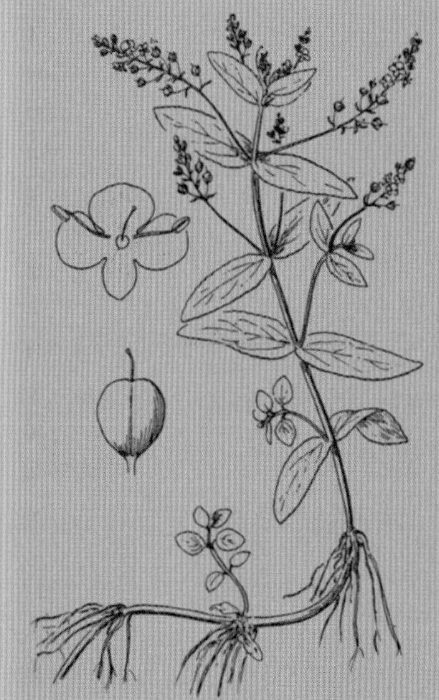

Great Water Speedwell, *Veronica anagallis-aquatica*

February - Migration & Reflections

Location: Palo Alto Baylands

Enrichment Evening: 7 – 9 p.m.

Speaker: Our baylands guide returns with slides telling the story of migration, and revealing the great increase in the waterfowl population since our autumn exploration. We learn that migration is an intricate rhythm in the natural world, orchestrated in a distinct place, yet performed throughout various habitats. Migratory species arrive at predestined stopovers primed for respite. Following their sojourn, the return home is inevitable. Each year, numerous species engage in this concert utilizing bioregions, such as those found in the greater Bay Area, as their stage — from northern elephant seals and gray whales to monarch butterflies, ladybird beetles and birds on the Pacific Flyway.

Introduction Question: Share an experience you have had of migration.

Materials: February schedule and description, maps, resources, articles and Ohlone story

Field Exploration: 9 a.m. – 3 p.m.

Back at Palo Alto Baylands Nature Preserve, one of the premier birding locations of the entire West Coast, we experience this place as winter turns to spring and birds begin to nest. In the morning, we are with a nature sensory awareness guide for our reflections segment of the day. We spend some time in a silent, solo walk to a spot where we can sit and ponder our sense of place, reflect, write and draw. Today we try to be especially attentive to "whatever we come across," as directed by our guide. At lunch we share our experiences. In the afternoon, a naturalist joins us to refine our observation skills, and help us learn about the baylands as a migratory habitat full of resources for birds. We absorb the great expanse of this preserved marshland and the interaction of both migrant and residential birds with their habitat — seeing a snowy egret poised in its foraging stance, the food-sweeping bill of the avocet and the hovering American kestrel ready to pounce.

Coltsfoot, *Petasites frigidus palmatus*

March - Restoration & Preservation

Location: Arastradero Preserve

Enrichment Evening: 7 – 9 p.m.

Speakers: One speaker provides a PowerPoint presentation on general restoration and preservation principles, as well as recent stewardship projects at Arastradero Preserve. The second speaker tells the story of restoration at Foothills Park.

Introduction Question: Have you ever been inspired to care for a natural place?

Materials: February schedule and description, maps, resources, articles and Ohlone story.

Field Exploration: 9 a.m. – 3 p.m.

Arastradero Preserve is a beautiful mixture of rolling savannah grassland and broad-leaf evergreen forest. Wildlife abounds. It is not uncommon to see deer, bobcats, coyotes and many varieties of birds. It is also an area that was heavily logged and over-grazed, and shows evidence of multiple needs for restoration. In the morning, as we walk through riparian areas, woodlands and grasslands, and around the lake, we become aware of the native and non-native plants, including invasive species, and of the areas being restored.

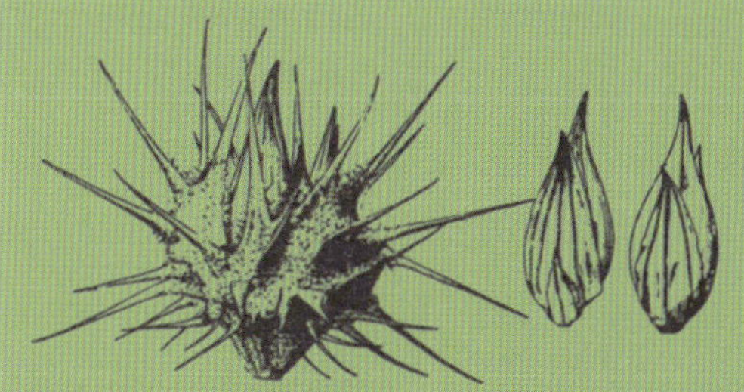

Mat Sandbur, *Cenchrus longispinus*

During lunch where the Acorn and Meadowlark trails meet, we enjoy a clear view across San Francisco Bay to the East Bay hills. Viewing these hills, it is apparent how the contours of the land direct water flowing down the hillsides and how watersheds form. After lunch we meet with one of the restoration directors, who walks us through various work sites. We finish the day with a hands-on restoration experience and appreciation of working together to restore our Earth.

April - Coming Home

Location: Windy Hill

Enrichment Evening: 7 – 9 p.m.

We gather around our campfire (tray of candles in a dark room) and learn together an indigenous chant in preparation for Saturday's sunrise. Then we spend the evening looking back at the journey we have taken together through the year. We share what has touched and changed us along the way, as well imagining our future journey forward. Later, in small groups, we make maps of our watershed and then present these to the larger group. For the last half hour, we gather around the campfire and invite each person to select a river stone from the fire circle. If they choose, participants add symbols, words or drawings to their stones. We close our evening with each person telling why they picked their particular stone and what, if anything, they drew or wrote on it. Everyone takes their stones with them as a symbol of the year's exploration of a sense of place. (Another year for our coming home evening, we set up the room with 12 stations around the walls, one for each month of the past year, and festooned the stations with pictures, artifacts and other reminders of each month's activities.)

Introduction Question: Over our yearlong exploration, is there a place you have felt a special connection to?

Deepening Exercise: Sharing around the campfire.

Materials: Evaluation form, plus April schedule and description, maps, resources, articles and Ohlone story.

Field Exploration:

Special time: 5:00 – 11:30 a.m.

Sunrise!

This day we come full circle. We return to the top of Windy Hill, where we began, but this time very early to witness the sunrise. Starting together in the murky dark of early morning, we experience the world around us gradually being revealed, and then greet the sun, the birds and other wildlife. Our guide leads us in the native sunrise chant we learned together as we find ourselves poised at the beginning of a new day, as well as at the beginning of spring — a time of hope and new possibilities. We take time to relate to this now-familiar place on our own, and also to breakfast and celebrate together!

Baylands

Painting by Wileta Burch, Palo Alto

Wileta Burch, a participant in the first Exploring a Sense of Place course, was inspired to try her hand at painting her bioregion, and develop her gifts as an artist. She says of her experience: "As I have become rooted in this Bay Area place, I have gained a deep love and appreciation for the natural world. I love the hills as they green in the springtime, the coast redwoods and magnificent oaks. Our bioregion is the most diverse in the world. From coast to bay and into the foothills we move through different climate zones and an amazing diversity of flora and fauna. Painting for me is one of the ways I try to become ever more connected to this place. My hope is that as one of many species that inhabit this precious land, we will treat the Earth with care and respect and leave it in good and bountiful shape for the children and grandchildren of all species to come."

Information
Worksheets & Checklists

WORKSHEETS & CHECKLISTS
SAMPLE COURSE DESIGN TIMELINE

1. Recruit your leadership team members

- ❑ Identify possible team members and the strengths they bring to the group.
- ❑ Define roles & assign titles.
- ❑ Hold an informational meeting for potential team members.
- ❑ Set a team meeting schedule.

WHEN: At least 6 months before start of course.

WHO: Course Leader

2. Recruit sponsors and advisors

- ❑ Develop relationships with people and institutions who can assist you.

WHEN: 5 months before start of course.

WHO: Course Leader, Team

3. Establish guidelines for your course

- ❑ Set course length and frequency and structure (e.g., one Saturday and one weekday evening per month for 12 months).
- ❑ Set class size depending on resources and facilities available. (Parks & preserves have limits to the number of persons who can enter at a time, typically 25-30.)
- ❑ Consider how much you need to charge for the course in order to cover any expenditures. (This will vary depending on your circumstances.)
- ❑ Estimate revenue & expenditures to generate a budget. Include costs for speakers'/docents' honoraria and materials, and a "miscellaneous" category for the inevitable unplanned costs.

WHEN: 5 months before start of course.

WHO: Team

4. Develop course timeline

- ❑ Fill in boxes similar to this sample.
- ❑ Add any steps that you and the team feel are missing.
- ❑ Be realistic about timelines, and refine as you proceed.

WHEN: 5 months before start of course.

WHO: Course Leader (or Program Manager) & Team Members

5. Do exploratory research on your bioregion

- ❑ Define your bioregion by tracing your watershed and identifying weather patterns.
- ❑ Identify knowledgeable people for each theme (speakers, docents, guides and storytellers). Get contact info and start a "contact file."
- ❑ Explore themes, assign team members to find resources for each theme.
- ❑ Identify indigenous peoples and first settlers of your area.
- ❑ Develop a filing library/system to collect relevant information and resources.
- ❑ Collect ideas for "deepening experiences" and exercises.

WHEN: 4 to 5 months before start of course.

WHO: All team members, perhaps in designated subcommittees

6. Establish means of communication

- ❑ Explore with team the most effective ways for the team to communicate. (Email? Listserv? Phone?) Put it into effect.
- ❑ Determine communication pathways for the course participants. (Mail? Listserv?)
- ❑ Have a backup plan for communication in case of technological failure.

WHEN: 3 months before start of course.

WHO: Team member with technical ability and team.

COURSE DESIGN TIMELINE

6 months prior to program start — **1.**

5 months — **2.** **3.** **4.** **5.**

3 months — **6.**

SAMPLE COURSE DESIGN TIMELINE - CONTINUED

7. Putting it all together

- ❑ Set calendar and schedule of places & themes for the entire course.
- ❑ Obtain any required permits or permission.
- ❑ Contact and schedule guides, speakers, etc., for each segment of the course (as possible).
- ❑ Plan materials and handouts.
- ❑ Set up administrative process. Develop program forms and checklist (see samples that follow).
- ❑ Finalize budget and course fees. Try for more than breakeven to have some cash on hand to start next course. (Open bank account if appropriate).

WHEN: 1 month before start of course (as required).

WHO: Team members as designated, with Team.

8. Recruit course participants

❑ Have each team member personally invite potential attendees.

WHEN: 3 to 4 weeks in advance.

WHO: Team members and Program Manager as designated.

❑ Develop advertising materials (newspaper ads, flyers, brochures).

WHEN: At least 1 month in advance.

WHO: Team members and Program Manager as designated.

❑ Print and distribute advertising materials.

WHEN: 3 – 4 weeks before start date.

WHO: Team members and Program Manager as designated.

❑ Generate registration system, forms and informational packets (to hand out at Introductory Evenings).

WHEN: 1 month before.

WHO: Team members and Program Manager as designated.

❑ Develop Web site information/text (if applicable).

WHEN: At least 4-6 weeks before start.

WHO: Team members and Program Manager as designated.

9. Hold Introductory Evenings (or Open Houses)

This is a way to advertise and recruit new participants, and to give them their first orientation to a Sense of Place. Be ready to register people on the spot.

WHEN:

Plan: 3-4 weeks ahead.

Hold: 1 and 2 weeks before start.

WHO: Team members and Program Manager as designated.

10. Prepare for Participants

- ❑ Compile course participant roster.
- ❑ Send out welcome/confirmation letters.
- ❑ Duplicate and prepare course materials once number of attendees is known.
- ❑ Assemble course notebooks or materials.
- ❑ Create participant listserv (if using).
- ❑ Compose email reminder announcement and send out to class participants.

WHEN: One week prior to class.

WHO: Team members or Program Manager as designated.

YOU ARE LAUNCHED!

NEXT STEPS: Prepare each program day.

1 month

7. 8. 9.

1 week

10.

Program Starts !

MONTHLY TEAM PLANNING GUIDE

The purpose of this team is to work together to create a cohesive, cumulative experience that will enhance the participants' sense of place. Ideally each member takes on a particular aspect of the project, doing something they enjoy, and with good communication and coordination, together the team will build a complete, rich program.

Monthly program responsibilities:

Once the schedule, locations and themes have been set, and a general structure of the explorations agreed upon, the planning work for monthly programs can be done. To carry out this task, two team members (one of whom takes prime responsibility) are assigned to each month, planning both the enrichment evening and Saturday exploration. These two report to the Program Manager and work in concert with him/her and the rest of the team for program planning, coordination and cohesiveness, and to ask for help as needed.

TASKS

1. Guides

- ❑ Obtain knowledgeable guides for the Saturday exploration (at least 2, and depending on group size maybe more).
- ❑ Have a conversation with them so that they understand the program's objective and the spirit of what we are doing, and listen to what they have in mind to enhance your program.
- ❑ Together with them, work out the schedule for the day, and the route you will take. This is best accomplished by doing a preplanning hike or walk of the area together if possible.
- ❑ Reconfirm with them shortly before both the enrichment evening and the exploration day (via email or phone – 2 to 3 days before), and coordinate any additional arrangements.
- ❑ Arrange with Program Manager regarding the guide's honorarium (if applicable).
- ❑ Follow up with note of appreciation and thanks, and ask for networking references.
- ❑ Be sure you have all the contact information, including any references, and forward to the Program Manager to add to the files, or for follow-up.

2. Program

- ❑ Plan program, keeping in mind theme, location, season, weather, opportunities for deepening experiences and participants.
- ❑ Coordinate plan with your other team members (at team meetings).
- ❑ Also plan the opening circle, a welcome and introduction to the day and closing circle that will enhance our appreciation of the day.

3. Site Logistics

- ❑ Plan route and logistics of site (where to start and finish, park, shuttles, restroom availability, etc.).
- ❑ Determine if a permit is necessary.
- ❑ Write a description and schedule for the day, and list of what to bring.
- ❑ Encourage or help organize carpooling arrangements.
- ❑ Prepare and bring to exploration day:
    - ❑ Maps, permit, directions, check-in sheet, pen, nametags
    - ❑ First aid kit, water and cell phone.

4. Materials

- ❑ Gather related resources for your program resource files, and select appropriate materials to include in participant notebooks as handouts.
- ❑ Check with Program Manager for materials already on file.
- ❑ Together with the Program Manager, decide on handouts and notebook materials.
- ❑ Reproduce and put together participant packets, including schedule, maps, resources, indigenous peoples' stories.

5. Communication (may be assigned to the Program Manager)

- ❑ Send description and schedule to participants' email list the week before the exploration, reminding them of the enrichment evening and stimulating interest in the program.

TEAM RESPONSIBILITIES

Enrichment Evening

❑ Secure a room to accommodate the program and size of the group.

ROOM PREPARATION

❑ Audio visual
(check with speaker ahead of time for needs, arrange for equipment.)
- VHS/DVD equipment?
- Overhead projector?
- Slide show equipment?
- Computer projector or slide projector?

❑ Chairs (set up facing front or side of room, circle?)

❑ Displays (bioregion or watershed map for reference and context, other posters or books?)

❑ Refreshments (designate who brings them ahead of time)

PREPARE AND PROVIDE:

❑ Participant packets

❑ Additional handouts (if any)

❑ Nametags

❑ Attendance sheet (check people in as they arrive so we know who picked up their packets)

❑ Money box to collect visitor fees

Saturday Exploration

❑ The safety and satisfactory experience of each and every participant is the primary objective of the whole team. Every member plays a variety of roles when participating in the Saturday explorations: leader, participant, docent, timekeeper and shepherd. A team member's role will differ from month to month depending on the level of his/her involvement in the development of the activities for that particular day. For example, if you were one of the two team members heading up that month's activities – your role would be greater for timekeeping and making sure the day unfolds as planned. If you are a "general team member" for that exploration, your role would be more supportive and alert to the welfare of individual participants. (Are they getting tired? Need a rest or to get moving more?)

❑ It is the responsibility of all team members to ensure the safety of course participants. Participants should not be allowed to leave the group early or decide to stay back from a group activity without permission from a team member. If a participant wants to skip or sit out part of the day, they must be accompanied by a team member at all times. (In other words: No one goes it alone and communication between team members is a must!)

❑ Though we recommend that participants leave cell phones and pagers at home so that they have an uninterrupted experience in nature, team members who have them should carry a cell phone in case of emergency. Beforehand, prepare emergency cards with all team cell numbers (and local emergency numbers), and distribute them at the start of each exploration. (Hint: These can be laminated and reused each month. Keep them with the first aid kit between explorations.) Identify team members with a special hat or name badge so that they will be easily identifiable to others in the group.

Further tips for success

❑ At the orientation to the course, let people know how much physical activity there will be so they can plan for it.

❑ Make it fun! For example, when the weather might be wet or cold, hold a fun, informal fashion show to demonstrate all-weather gear. (Emphasize layers that can be added or removed.)

❑ Include active and still times when planning explorations. Combine standing, walking and sitting time so there is a good balance. (Suggest bringing lightweight campstools for those who tire of standing.)

❑ Have some quiet time (periods without talking so that you can better take in the surroundings) and time to connect with each other.

❑ Plan an activity where the group does some nature restoration work together if possible. (Contact a conservation organization in your area for guidance.) This is most effective toward the end of the course when the group is more knowledgeable about what is needed in your area. They usually find it very gratifying to be able to respond, even in a small way, to these needs.

❑ Have a first aid kit and water along with you for every exploration outdoors. Someone on the team should be trained in basic first aid.

❑ Have participants sign a release form.

❑ Be sure that there is access to restrooms at some point in the exploration, and design the day so that you don't have to go too long between restroom breaks.

MONTHLY CHECKLIST

Part 1: ENRICHMENT EVENING

Date: ______________ Location: ______________________________

Theme: ____

Name of speaker: ______________________________________

Contact information (phone & email): ______________________

Time speaker to arrive: ________________________________

Special equipment needs:
- ❏ VCR/TV
- ❏ DVD player
- ❏ Overhead projector
- ❏ Slide projector
- ❏ PowerPoint setup (laptop, projector, etc.)
- ❏ Screen
- ❏ Tape/CD player
- ❏ Podium or tables

Standard meeting supplies:
- ❏ Nametags
- ❏ Attendance sheet & course roster (pens, pencils)
- ❏ Handouts/materials (schedule, maps, directions, articles, etc.)
- ❏ Easel and flip chart (pens)
- ❏ Watershed chart on easel

❏ Other: ____

Coordinating team members: ____________________________

Team member assignments: _____________________________

AV and other equipment checkout: ________________________

Room setup and clean up: ______________________________

AV setup and take down: _______________________________

Refreshments: _______________________________________

Program assignments: _________________________________

Welcome and review of last month: _______________________

Introductory question: _________________________________

Introduction of this month's theme: _______________________

Materials review and Saturday logistics: ___________________

Introduction of speaker: _______________________________

Closing: ____

Part 2: EXPLORATION DAY

Carpool location & time: _______________________________

Site location, directions & meeting time: ___________________

Description & schedule: ________________________________

Team member coordinating day: __________________________

Docent/guide: ______________________ Phone# _______________

Docent/guide: ______________________ Phone# _______________

Opening: ____

Closing: ____

Items to bring:
- ❏ Attendance sheet & course roster
- ❏ Clipboard/pens
- ❏ Nametags
- ❏ First aid kit
- ❏ Extra water
- ❏ Maps & materials
- ❏ Cell phone # ________________ Name: ________________

  # ________________ Name: ________________

TIPS FOR ORGANIZING EXPLORATORY RESEARCH FILES

In planning any program, it is valuable to do research. Early on, Exploring a Sense of Place founders set up a filing system with folders to help collect and organize relevant articles, pictures, maps and other information on a variety of subjects. Folders were made for each of the monthly themes we were considering, the locations we would visit and all of the subjects that would make up this exploration. These files helped us immensely as we shaped our program, and became the source of much of the supplementary material for the participants' notebooks each month. By setting them up beforehand, you will find that these categories can also help guide and stimulate your research as you explore the many aspects of your Place. By the time your course is implemented, you will probably have much more material than you can use in the allotted time, but it could be made available to participants who want to delve more deeply into any one subject.

Below is our list of subject headings. We recommend that you set up your own similar files. After a period of exploratory research, you might find that some folders are overflowing, some are nearly empty and you might need to add some new ones. You will also have a wealth of wonderful material for your course.

SAMPLE FILE TOPICS

Big Picture

Solar System and Cosmology (sunset, stargazing)
Earth Charter (human response)

Bioregion

Definition
Maps

Climate/Weather

Contacts

People Resources (possible guides, naturalists, storytellers, docents, rangers...)

Deepening Our Connection

Coming Home (sunrise celebration)
Creativity in Nature

Inspiration/Reflections

Poetry/music/dance
Sensory exercises (touch, taste, sight, sound, taste and...)

Ecology

Food: Local, Seasonal and Organic
Foothills and Oak Savannah

Geology

Human Impact

Current Issues
"Heroes and Sheroes" (e.g., foresighted, courageous folks who have defended, preserved and restored the local ecology as parks and open space)
History of Place
Human Systems Water and Waste
Native Peoples' Story
Restoration and Preservation

Maps & Locations

(Particulars of sites to visit)
Arastradero Preserve
Foothill Park
Hidden Villa
Huddart Park
Jasper Ridge Preserve
Palo Alto Baylands
Russian Ridge Preserve
San Francisquito Creek
Windy Hill Preserve

Plants

Natives / Invasives
Threatened / Endangered
Wildflowers, Grasses, Trees

Seasonal Change

Watershed

High Watershed and Coastal Mountains
Lower Watershed and Riparian Environment

Ponds and Lakes
Streams

Wildlife

Amphibians / Fish / Reptiles
Birds / Migrations and Reflections
Insects / Microbes
Habitats
Mammals Large/Small
Natives and Invasives
Threatened / Endangered
Tracking (wildlife tracking)

Life of a Raindrop

Raindrop born
of formless vapors,
first aware of swirling air,
being drawn it knows
not where,
faster, faster, on it plunges,
until it slides down
a blade of grass
and seeps in mountain earth
at last.

Raindrop makes its way
through soil,
ever pulled by unseen force,
joins with other newborns
like it,
then on through life,
a patterned course of
stagnant pauses,
breathless rapids,
playful ripples, joyful splashes,
dizzy eddies, painful tumbles,
branching choices,
sudden stumbles.

Raindrop passes from that life,
back to gases whence it came
to fall on yet another peak,
perhaps a roof
or upturned cheek,
again, again, and yet again —
now a flash to quench
the desert,
now sucked up by cells of wheat,
now a rinse for city streets.

Raindrop flows
in seamless cycles,
bound to join the boundless sea.

MIKE ABKIN
SENSE OF PLACE
PALO ALTO

YOUR NOTES & IDEAS

Information

Registration & Organizational Materials

REGISTRATION & ORGANIZATIONAL MATERIALS EXAMPLE

EXPLORING A SENSE OF PLACE
REGISTRATION FORM
MAY 2006 – APRIL 2007

Please register me for Exploring a Sense of Place Series:

Name: ______________________________

Address: ______________________________

City: ______________________ State: ________ ZIP: __________

Phone: (H) ____________________ (W) ____________________

Please Print Clearly!

Email: ______________________________

This is our main form of communication – we will not share your email with anyone else.

FEES

Note: The $375 registration fee covers the entire yearlong program, including 12 Saturday Explorations, 12 Enrichment evenings, notebook materials, maps, docents, special guides, entrance fees. Enrollment is limited to 30 participants; course will be filled on a first-come, first-served basis from paid participants with a preference to full-year registrations.

Registration Fee: Full year: $375 ____________________
(Couples discount of $50, or $350 each, share one notebook.)

As space is available, you may sign up on a half-year basis @ $200

______ May - October

______ November - April

#______________________________ Exp. Date __________

We accept American Express, MasterCard, Discover, and Visa

Signature ______________________________

Person filling out form/initials: ____________________ Date: __________

If by mail, please return to:

EXPLORING A SENSE OF PLACE
1023 Corporation Way
Palo Alto, CA 94303

call 650-938-9300

Enclosed Checks, please make payable to "Exploring a Sense of Place – Conexions"

Exploring a Sense of Place

Acknowledgment of Participant Responsibility, Express Assumption of Risk, and Release of Liability

I understand that during my participation in Exploring a Sense of Place Field Explorations — scheduled in the period from April 2006 through May 2007 — I may be exposed to a variety of hazards and risks, foreseen or unforeseen, which are inherent in each Exploration and cannot be eliminated without destroying the unique character of the exploration. These inherent risks include, but are not limited to, the dangers of serious personal injury, property damage, and death ("Injuries and Damages") from exposure to the hazards of travel. Exploring a Sense of Place has not tried to contradict or minimize my understanding of these risks. I know that Injuries and Damages can occur by natural causes or activities of other persons, animals, trip members, trip leaders and assistants, or third parties, either as a result of negligence or because of other reasons. I understand that risks of such Injuries and Damages are involved in adventure travel such as Exploring a Sense of Place Explorations and I appreciate that I may have to exercise extra care for my own person and for others around me in the face of such hazards. I further understand that on these Explorations there may not be rescue or medical facilities or expertise necessary to deal with the Injuries and Damages to which I may be exposed.

In consideration for my acceptance as a participant on these Explorations, and the services and amenities to be provided by Exploring a Sense of Place in connection with these Explorations, I confirm my understanding that:

I have read any rules and conditions applicable to the Explorations made available to me; I will pay any costs and fees for the Explorations; and I acknowledge my participation is at the discretion of the leaders.

The Explorations officially begin and end at the location(s) designated by Exploring a Sense of Place. The Explorations do not include carpooling, transportation, or transit to and from the Explorations, and I am personally responsible for all risks associated with this travel. This does not apply to transportation provided by Exploring a Sense of Place during the Exploration.

If I decide to leave early and not to complete the Explorations as planned, I assume all risks inherent in my decision to leave and waive all liability against Exploring a Sense of Place arising from that decision. Likewise, if a leader concludes a particular Exploration, and I decide to go forward without the leader, I assume all risks inherent in my decision to go forward and waive all liability against Exploring a Sense of Place arising from that decision.

This Agreement is intended to be as broad and inclusive as is permitted by law. If any provision or any part of any provision of this Agreement is held to be invalid or legally unenforceable for any reason, the remainder of this Agreement shall not be affected thereby and shall remain valid and fully enforceable.

To the fullest extent allowed by law, I agree to WAIVE, DISCHARGE CLAIMS, AND RELEASE FROM LIABILITY Exploring a Sense of Place, its officers, directors, employees, agents, and leaders from any and all liability on account of, or in any way resulting from Injuries and Damages in any way connected with Explorations. I further agree to HOLD HARMLESS Exploring a Sense of Place, its officers, directors, employees, agents, and leaders from any claims, damages, injuries, or losses caused by my own negligence while a participant on the outings. I understand and intend that this assumption of risk and release is binding upon my heirs, executors, administrators, and assigns, and includes any minors accompanying me on the Explorations.

I have read this document in its entirety and I freely and voluntarily assume all risks of such Injuries and Damages and notwithstanding such risks, I agree to participate in these Explorations.

______________________________ ______________________

Signature Date

LEGAL & FINANCIAL TIPS

from Cindy Spring, Coordinator, Close to Home

Legal & Financial Considerations

If one is setting up a Sense of Place program from scratch, without the benefit of an existing organization as an umbrella, there are several legal and financial considerations.

1. Legal entity: In California, an entity that takes money for goods or services must at a minimum be registered in the county within which it is doing business. The cofounders went to the county clerk's office and completed a "dba" ("Doing Business As") form. We first had to give them our organization name, and they did a quick check to see if anyone else in the county had that name taken. Fortunately for us, no one had. Then we filled out a form that requested basic information on the two cofounders. The cost of that filing was $35. The next step is to publish this as a legal notice. We went to the local newspaper with the county form, and it was published four times. This is a very common process, and the newspaper handled it easily. The cost was around $25. A few weeks later we received our official notice that we were a legal entity.

2. Bank account: The bank accepted the official dba form, and we were able to open a checking account with both names of cofounders. One of the cofounders agreed to handle the account.

3. Tax considerations: One of the two cofounders had a sole proprietorship company for which she filled a Schedule C form each year. Having such a company allows one to deduct business expenses from income. She added a second Schedule C form for the new entity and claimed all income and deductions. Since the income and deductions for the Sense of Place program were very closely matched, there was a negligible effect on her income tax statement.

YOUR NOTES & IDEAS

Information
Sample Notebook Materials

SAMPLE NOTEBOOK MATERIALS

FROM OCTOBER, SENSE OF PLACE

Exploring a Sense of Place
Month 6
Saturday, October 22, 2005

Place: Palo Alto Baylands Natural Preserve
Theme: Life in an Estuary

Enrichment Evening: Monday, October 17, 7 – 9 PM

Tonight's guest is the City of Palo Alto's Naturalist, Deborah Bartens. Deborah is responsible for all of the City's open space parks: Palo Alto Baylands, Foothill Park, and Arastradero Preserve. She has worked as a ranger and a naturalist for the City for almost 20 years. She is a rare treasure and we are pleased that she has been part of our program for the past four years.

Exploration Day: Saturday October 22, 9:00 AM – 3:00 PM

Description of the Day: The Palo Alto Baylands are cared for and preserved by the City of Palo Alto. Consisting of over 1,600 acres of protected land, the preserve includes some of the last remaining salt marsh/mudflat habitats on the West Coast. It is home to the endangered California clapper rail and the salt marsh harvest mouse. Deborah Bartens is the official steward of the Baylands and is an avid birder who will share some of the area's best-kept secrets with us while on our journey.

We will start the day at the Lucy Evans Baylands Nature Interpretive Center and meet up with Deborah. There we will explore and experience the different wildlife displays within the Interpretive Center, as well as going on our walk beside the Bay.

Deborah will introduce us to the different vegetation growing within the mudflats and point out some of the various birds that are migrating though the area. Low tide for the day will be at 11:39 AM, with the tide rising again in the late afternoon before we leave.

During lunch, we will have time to rest in the shade and enjoy your refreshments while discussing the "Bioregional Quiz." (Hint: Check it out before Saturday — it's in your notebook under the orientation section.) Let's see how much we have learned in the first six months of Sense of Place!

After lunch, we will continue our journey with Sense of Place team member David Coale, who will lead us to the mouth of the San Francisquito Creek. From this vantage point, we can see to the west the entire sweep of our Sense of Place explorations thus far: from Windy Hill, through the oak-studded foothills, and along the path of San Francisquito Creek where we walked in July. And if the tide is low enough, we might be able to see some debris (large tree limbs and/or large rocks, or who knows what?) that has made that same journey too! To finish our day, we will do some bird watching on the way back to our cars.

Schedule

8:45 to 9:00	Self-organized carpooling from FGC. Nature Center parking area is currently closed for renovation, please park near the Duck Pond area.
9:15 to 9:30	Meet in front of the Baylands Nature Interpretive Center
9:30 to 11:30	Discovery in the Interpretive Center & exploration of the Bay with Deborah Bartens.
11:30 to 1:00	Group lunch and Bioregional Quiz
1:00 to 3:00	Walk to the mouth of the Bay & San Francisquito Creek Bay bird watching.

What to bring

- No-waste picnic lunch
- Water to drink
- Dress in layers, especially for a cool wind
- Sun protection (including a hat)
- Sturdy shoes
- Binoculars
- Bird book or shorebird cards for identification

EXPLORING A SENSE OF PLACE

Life in an Estuary – Palo Alto Baylands

Monday, October 17, 2005
7 to 9 PM

Agenda

7:00 to 7:15	Welcome and review of last month (Hidden Villa) – (Leslie)
7:15 to 7:40	Introductory exercise – (Julie) "Is there a bay, estuary or marsh experience that you can remember?"
7:40 to 7:45	Introduction of this month's theme (David) (Watershed Map Overview & Orientation Palo Alto Baylands)
7:45 to 8:00	Saturday's logistics and cool weather fashion show (Julie & Gail)
8:00 to 9:00	Presentation and slide show by Deborah Bartens
Refreshments:	Jill – Chocolate Karen – Fruit Leslie – Popcorn Lemonade in refridge.

Trust

To trust not trusting
Now release
grasp his hand
the world to be shown you
is your own
you will not know how you can
be until
crest the hill
view the world below
amber fields
cool lakes
heaven beckons
the stars glimmer down
up
don't know knowing
be

JULIE GOOD
SENSE OF PLACE, PALO ALTO

Indigenous People Story for October

An Ohlone Village by the Bay

The village is located at the mouth of a freshwater creek. An immense, sprawling pile of shells, earth, and ashes elevates the site above the surrounding marshland. On top of this mound stand some fifteen dome-shaped tule houses arranged around a plaza-like clearing. Scattered among them are smaller structures that look like huge baskets on stilts — granaries in which the year's supply of acorns is stored.

It is mid-afternoon of a clear, warm day. In several places throughout the village, steam is rising from underground pit ovens where mussels, clams, rabbit meat, fish, and various roots are being roasted for the evening meal. People are clustered near the doors of the houses. Three men sit together, repairing a fishing net. A group of children are playing an Ohlone version of hide-and-seek. Here and there an older person is lying face down on a woven tule mat, napping in the afternoon sun.

At the edge of the village, a group of women sit together grinding acorns. Holding the mortars between their outstretched legs, they sway back and forth, raising the pestles and letting them fall again. The women are singing together, and the pestles rise and fall in unison. As heavy as the pestles are, they are lifted easily, not so much by muscular effort, but (it seems to the women) by the powerful rhythm of the acorn-grinding songs. The singing of the women and the synchronized thumping of a dozen stone pestles create a familiar background noise, a noise that has been heard by the people of this village every day for hundreds, maybe thousands, of years.

The women are dressed in skirts of tule reeds and deerskin. They are muscular, with rounded healthy features. They wear no shoes or sandals — neither do the men — and their feet are hardened by a lifetime of walking barefoot. Tattoos, mostly lines and dots, decorate their chins, and they are wearing necklaces made of abalone shells, clamshell beads, olivella shells, and feathers.

On a warm day like this, almost all village activity takes place outdoors, for the tule houses are rather small. Of relatively simple design (they are made by fastening bundles of tule rush onto a framework of bent willow poles), they range in size from six to about 20 feet in diameter. The larger dwellings hold one or sometimes two families, as many as 12 or more people, and each house is crowded with possessions. Blankets of deerskin, bearskin, and woven rabbitskin lie strewn about a central fire pit. Hamper baskets in which seeds, roots, dried meat, and dried fish are stored stand against the smoke-darkened walls. Winnowing, serving, sifting, and cooking baskets, along with several unfinished baskets in various stages of completion, are stacked near the entrance way. Many of the houses also contain ducks stuffed with tule (to be used as hunting decoys), piles of fishing nets, fish traps, snares, clay balls ready to be ground into paint, and heaps of abalone shells that have been worked into rough blanks. The abalone shells were received in trade last fall from the people across the Bay, and after being shaped, polished, and pierced they will eventually be traded eastward — for pine nuts, everyone hopes.

The women have finished grinding their acorns. They pile fresh wood into their outdoor cooking fires, leach the acorn meal with hot water, and begin to make the mush that will form the basis for the night's dinner.

The villagers eat in groups around the various houses. The meals are noisy, full of jokes and good humor. People exchange stories of the day's activities. A lazy woman who has ground her acorns badly and an inept fisherman who has not caught any fish are teased by everyone, as they have been teased many times before. The people dip two fingers into their bowls of acorn gruel and slurp up more of the rich, bland food. Clamshells, mussel shells, and animal bones are tossed into a pile beyond the circle of houses.

As it gets dark, the infants and toddlers crawl in among the blankets to go to sleep. Others put on rabbitskin capes or wrap themselves in deerskin blankets. The older children gather around their grandfathers and grandmothers, hoping for a story.

Several men have gone to the sweathouse. They've eaten acorn food only and will spend the entire night in the sweathouse. The next day, if their dreams are favorable, they will don their deer-head masks to seek deer. In the sweathouse tonight, they will tell hunting stories, smoke tobacco, and perhaps dream the right dreams. If the dreams are favorable, tomorrow they will light fires in the sweathouse again, sweat some more, paint their bodies, put on their deer-head masks, and go out to hunt.

The other people in the village smile. Perhaps tomorrow there will be fresh deer meat. That is good, very good. Everyone will get some. But more than that, if the men head out into the hills, they will bring back news about the flower seeds. Perhaps the chief will give the word to move outward into the hills where the people can throw themselves face down onto the slopes and eat the delicious clover, and where they can taste again the nutty, roasted kernels of buttercup, clarkia, and redmaid seeds. The people feel glad inside just thinking about it. It has been a good day and they will soon retire for the night.

Excerpts from "An Ohlone Village," pages 13 – 22, The Ohlone Way, Indian Life in the San Francisco-Monterey Bay Area, *by Malcolm Margolin, Heyday Books, 1978.*

Sample Local Information Sheets

Every month in our notebooks, we provide relevant nature, ecology or species articles from local environmental or science newsletters, as well as maps, reading lists and other educational materials. For this October notebook addition, we included articles on two endangered wetland species, the salt marsh harvest mouse and California clapper rail, copied from a Nature Notes newsletter produced about the Palo Alto baylands by the city's community services department. We also included this detailed trail and access map to our exploration destination.

Palo Alto

BAYLANDS

California Clapper Rail

Nature Notes

The California Clapper Rail is a small brownish marsh bird 14 to 16.6 inches long with a slender body and relatively long legs. It has a buff colored front and white bars or stripes on its sides. The bird's two and a half inch long beak is relatively thick and curves downward to aid in feeding. The Rail has developed stout feet with long toes for walking on mud. Normally a very shy and secretive bird, the Clapper Rail can occasionally be seen carefully picking its way along the tidal channels of the marshland searching for food. The Rail eats a number of small sized marsh creatures including *polychaete* worms, snails, crabs and other crustaceans, insects, spiders, small mammals like mice, and an occasional small fish.

Cautious by nature, Rails rarely venture from the safety of their hiding places in the marsh grass. The best time of the year to view Clapper Rails is during winter's high tides, when the birds are flooded out of low areas of the marshlands. Though capable of limited flight, Rails rarely fly and prefer to swim or wade when crossing tidal channels. If startled, the Rail typically darts away over the ground and hides in nearby cordgrass or pickleweed. Its position is sometimes given away by the bird's habit of quickly flicking its tail or by its clapping call.

The Clapper Rail's nest is well hidden among the marsh plant growth, and is woven of pickleweed and cord grass. These materials enable the bowl shaped nest to float in the high tides of early summer, and will protect the eggs and chicks from the rising water. Between late March and July, the California Clapper will lay an average of 8 to 10 eggs. The 1 to 1.5 inch long eggs are a light buff or cream color with varying amounts of brown spots. Both parents take turns incubating the eggs, a process that lasts from 21 to 23 days. The downy chicks appear from April to August and are solid black in color.

The Clapper Rail has a number of native predators, including some birds of prey. Harriers, Red-tailed Hawks and Peregrine Falcons have been seen feeding on adult Rails. Nests often fall victim to the Norway Rat, a rodent that eats both the eggs and the chicks. The non-native Red Fox has also become a major threat to the dwindling Rail population.

Many natural predators have contributed to the Rail population decline in the San Francisco Bay. But the major reason is the decrease of their habitat by 85 percent since the turn of the century due to marshland development. Unfortunately Rails are only able to survive in salt marshes. As of January 1993 there were only 81 California Clapper Rails recorded in the Palo Alto Baylands Nature Preserve.

The Clapper Rail's original range was from Marin County to Los Angeles. Now, it can really only be found within the salt marshes of San Francisco Bay. Two other Rail sub-species live in California, but they too are endangered.

Edited and Illustrated by Virginia Kolence

City of Palo Alto Department of Community Services

Palo Alto

BAYLANDS

Salt Marsh Harvest Mouse

Nature Notes

The Salt Marsh Harvest Mouse is found only within the salt marshes of San Francisco Bay. In addition to the Palo Alto Baylands marshes, it is also found in the marshes of Corte Madera, San Pablo, San Leandro, Fremont, Alviso, and Redwood City.

The Salt Marsh Harvest Mouse is a small brown mouse, 2.9 to 4.6 inches (75 to 117 mm) long from head to tail. They only weigh about a third of an ounce (9 to 11 grams), about as much as three copper pennies. Their most distinctive marking is a patch of red or cinnamon colored fur on the belly. Consequently, it has also been called the "Red-bellied Harvest Mouse."

It is extremely difficult to view a Salt Marsh Harvest Mouse because they are mostly nocturnal and live within the marsh pickleweed and cordgrass. The mice are active between dusk and about an hour after sunrise, spending the majority of this time searching for food. During high tides the mice commonly climb atop plants and bushes to keep dry. They are capable of swimming but rarely chose to do so. During the highest tides of December and January, they are forced to relocate temporarily to the more elevated areas of the marshland. So either of these tide conditions gives one the best chance of actually seeing this tiny mouse.

Though small, the Salt Marsh Harvest Mouse has a large appetite. Its basic diet is green or dry marsh vegetation, but it eats sizable quantities of seeds when they are available. It is a true herbivore and does not eat insects as do many other mice species. It is also one of the few animals in the world that can sustain itself on brackish water alone, but it usually prefers to drink dew drops.

The highest reproductive activity of the females takes place between March and November. A simple nest is built on the ground in less than half a night. Each female will have from 1 to 4 litters a year, with 2 to 4 babies in each. The mouse population fluctuates greatly on a seasonal basis. A peak occurs during the Spring and summer breeding periods. The population drops to a minimum in the Fall and winter months when the tides force the mice onto higher ground and more vulnerable positions.

The total number of Salt Marsh Harvest Mice remaining in the Palo Alto Baylands is unknown, but it is not a large population. They are eaten by a number of animals, including Short-eared Owls, Northern Harriers, American Kestrels, and even California Clapper Rails. They are listed as an endangered species, primarily because of the great loss of their marshland habitat in the Bay area over the last hundred years.

Edited and Illustrated by Virginia Kolence

City of Palo Alto Department of Community Services

October Resource List

Recommended Reading

Clark, Jeanne L. *California Wildlife Viewing Guide*. Falcon: 1996.

Emory, Jerry. *San Francisco Bay Shoreline Guide*. California State Coastal Conservancy: 1995.

Faber, Phyllis M. *Common Wetland Plants of Coastal California*. Pickleweed Press: 1996.

Faber, Phyllis M. and Robert Holland. *Common Riparian Plants of California*. Pickleweed Press: 1996.

Lukas, David. *Wild Birds of California*. Companion Press.

Web Sites

The Bay Trail
www.abag.ca.gov/bayarea/baytrail/baytrail.html
The Web site for the trail around the entire Bay — for the adventurous.

California Department of Fish and Game/Wildlife Areas and Ecological Preserves
www.dfg.ca.gov/lands/wa/index.htm
Good for information on fish and marine life in the Bay.

The History and Effects of Exotic Species in the San Francisco Bay
http://sfbay.wr.usgs.gov/access/exotic-species/index.html
A great visual tool for understanding the influx of non-native species.

Mercury Contamination from Historic Gold Mining in California
http://ca.water.usgs.gov/mercury
Discusses the issue of mercury runoff from gold mining that contaminated the Bay a century ago.

Haiku

So many yellow flowers
one bumblebee
and me.

Plain gray sky.
Good for seeing branches.

No sound
on this ground
amongst the trees.

MARIA GRANDINETTE
SENSE OF PLACE
PALO ALTO

Big Picture

As I journey along pursuing meaning and purpose, I stumble upon wonderful guide stones: experiences that reveal everything through a more clarifying and expanded lens. Perhaps the most illuminating of these has been an amazing big-picture view of our 13-billion-year evolutionary story. As I began to digest this story, I had several essential insights.

The first was a strong, reassuring sense that finally, what I was experiencing was "big enough." It was as if, without consciously realizing it, I had always been searching for a more adequate context for our lives, one that had sufficient scope in time as well as space. The universe story provided an inner assurance of a big enough scope to focus my life energy and fill the rest of my life, even though I might be just barely scratching the surface.

The second insight was a realization that I, along with everything else, already belong. At a subterranean level, I had been entangled in a pursuit of questioning: Do I belong to this family, this group, this institution? Through this expanded worldview, not only had the question of belonging been answered, but also the correlating task for each and everyone offered – the simple giving of oneself.

KAREN HARWELL
SENSE OF PLACE
PALO ALTO

YOUR NOTES & IDEAS

Information

Deepening Materials

DEEPENING MATERIALS

"The real voyage of discovery consists not in seeking new lands, but in seeing with new eyes." - Marcel Proust

These are examples of exercises that can be done to increase sensory awareness and the ability to see with new eyes and even hear with new ears. Good resources for such exercises that you can adapt for your Exploring a Sense of Place program are the many books by Joseph Cornell, who developed successful methods of connecting children and nature (see Resources, p. 89). Adults, too, can expand their awareness and nature appreciation through the ideas and inspiration in these books.

EXERCISE A: Diversity

As preparation for our Saturday exploration of a local ridge, take some time to spend in your yard (or somewhere outside) to do the following:

How many types of the following plants and animals do you see or suspect might be present?
If you don't know how many are present, then can you make a rough estimate?
If you know their names (common or species), feel free to list them.
If you don't know their names, try looking them up in a reference book.
Some of the items you find might be in overlapping categories.

Make a list of what you see!

Grasses:

Shrubs:

Trees:

Flowering Plants:

Birds:

Worms:

Spiders:

Other Insects:

EXERCISE B: Sense Meditation and Awareness Walk by Drew Harwell

I first learned this exercise while studying permaculture, a system of ecological design, in Arizona. On a one-hour night walk with our senses fully awake, we were able to gather an enormous amount of information about the site that was very useful in the creation of our design. My experience of this process has been greatly expanded since studying with naturalist and tracker Jon Young in the Regenerative Design and Nature Awareness yearlong training.

This exercise is a great way to have your participants explore their sense of place, literally. By opening up our senses, we allow the place to fully communicate with us. By practicing sense meditation and awareness walking, we can take in the big picture of what is happening in nature.

Sense Meditation

Begin by having the participants gather in a circle, about arm's length apart from each other. Give them any logistics they will need for the walk first, so that when you finish taking them through the sense meditation, you can move directly into the awareness walk.

Have everyone close their eyes and take a few deep breaths, feeling the air around them filling their lungs. This will also help them to relax and settle into their bodies. After a couple breaths, have them focus on their sense of smell. Breathe in and see how many different smells you can sense. Our sense of smell has been greatly reduced living in the modern world, so it is a good one to start exercising!

Next have them use their taste buds. Notice the tastes that are in the mouth from the meal they had earlier, or the sip of water they just took. Also, have them breathe through their mouth to taste the air. Our sense of smell and taste are very intertwined; remind them to keep aware of their sense of smell while we open our sense of taste.

Next have them focus on their body and skin. What sensations do they feel in their body? Are they standing in a comfortable way? Where on their body do they feel the warmth of the sun? Cold? Do they feel the wind? Ask a question about smells or taste to encourage them to stay in awareness of all the senses you have covered so far.

Next have them pay attention to all the sounds around them. What is the farthest sound you can hear? What is the closest sound you can hear? Instruct them to listen to sounds in all directions. Encourage them to listen to that farthest sound and the closest sound all at once. Are they still feeling the warmth of the sun?

Have them focus on awareness of all the above senses for about a minute before they open their eyes.

We tend to use our eyes to the exclusion of the other senses, so that is why we focus on them last in this exercise. Tell them that when they are ready to open their eyes, to use their peripheral vision. Have them put their fingers out to the side and wiggle them to see how wide their peripheral vision is. Where do they lose sight of their fingers? Have them play with the edge from side to side and up and down. Next, have them try to see everyone in the circle at the same time. Who is moving and who is standing still? Are they still paying attention to the sounds, smells, tastes and sensations of the skin?

Awareness Walk

After you have taken your participants through the sense meditation, you are ready to send them on a walk. I like to send them out one at a time spaced about 15 feet apart. During the walk, they are continuing the sense meditation they did in the circle. You have a few options with the walk. You can have a set place that they will all walk to, or have them wander at their own pace.

If they are walking to a set place, have a leader in the front who has been to the place before. Make sure participants know to give the person in front of them space, so they can relax into the experience. When they get to the gathering place, have them sit down and either continue the sense meditation, or write in their journals about their experience. This approach works well when you are trying to cover some ground or you have a narrow trail to walk. When choosing how far to walk, realize that walking with awareness usually slows people down. Think about how long it would take a seven-year-old to walk that distance.

If you are in a place that would allow for wandering, have a coyote or crow call that you can send out so the participants know when to return. The wandering approach can be used when you have a wide trail or a dirt road, or you are in an area where people can wander in multiple directions. If there is no destination, then it is easier for people to sink into the experience. Have a set time for them to wander, and then find a place to sit with awareness, and then journal. Repeat the coyote or crow call to bring them back in.

When you gather back as a group, allow time to debrief the experience. People usually have a lot to say, but if not, I ask some questions. "Where were you feeling curious?" "What was your internal experience while walking with awareness?" "What caught your attention?"

EXERCISE C: Hidden Pencil
By Derek Harwell

This activity is introduced as a game to challenge people's observation skills, but what it really does is challenge people's assumptions in their observations.

Materials: 1 pencil (optimally one that has a natural wood finish)

Time: 15 – 30 minutes

Space: 30 ft. x 30 ft. (ideally open forest floor with many twigs) outdoors

Number of People: 6 – 20

Optimal Age: 10 and up

The Game:

- Tell the group that you are going to play a game in order to test their powers of observation. You can introduce the idea by talking about adaptations and camouflage.
- Tell the group that you are going to hide the pencil somewhere in the defined area and that they are to find it.
- Once they find the pencil, they proceed to a predetermined place outside the area but do not let the others know where the pencil is.
- Demonstrate how they are not supposed to point to the pencil and say, "There's the pencil," which would give it away for others. If you demonstrate this by putting the pencil on the ground and pointing at it while exclaiming that you have found it, you will play on the assumptions of the group that the pencil will be on the ground.
- Have the group step outside of the area while you hide the pencil.
- Walk around to make it seem as though you are looking for a space to hide the pencil. Place the pencil behind your ear, so that it is plainly visible. Call the group back in to look.
- While they are looking, remind the group that when they find the pencil, they should not give it away to others. Remind them of this often.
- As a clue, you can ask people questions such that they look right at you.
- You will know when people have found it by their reaction. Sometimes kids will try to fake that they have found the pencil.
- You can also say things like, "The pencil has moved" or if you have asked everyone in the group a question and they have all looked at you, you can say, "Everyone here has looked right at the pencil."

Debrief:

- It is important to keep the debrief light, encourage people to laugh at themselves. Sometimes people can get a little upset or stuck on the notion that the game is not fair. It is important to acknowledge people's feelings but focus on why we played the game, which is to challenge our assumptions about how we see in nature. Remind them to look for the unexpected, and for things hidden in plain sight.
- Follow up on what people's assumptions were about where the pencil would be and why. Encourage them to think about what their other assumptions may be as they head into the natural world. What else might they miss by not overcoming those assumptions?

Variations:

- You can also play this game in 2-3 stages:
  - -stage 1 hide the pencil in the ground
  - -stage 2 hide the pencil off the ground (in a tree)
  - -stage 3 hide the pencil behind your ear
- This method is not as dramatic, but does help people build to the ultimate goal of shifting their focus from myopic to broad.

EXERCISE D: Creating a Sound Map
by Derek Harwell

This activity is introduced as a way to enhance people's awareness of bird and animal sounds and their proximity.

Materials for each participant: 1 pencil and a handful of colored pencils and a paper (or their journal).

Time: 45 minutes to 1 hour – After a brief instruction, send participants off for 30 minutes of listening and drawing and allow 15 minutes for sharing in the circle.

Space: An area large enough for participants to be able to fan out and find a spot to sit and listen.

The Experience

Explain to the group that we are going to engage in an activity that will enhance our ability to listen to and hear the sounds of the natural world. Invite people to wander out and find a setting where they can be quiet and begin their listening experience with their eyes closed.

We can often hear animals before we see them, and a good way to become aware of their existence in the area is to listen for their calls and the sounds of their movements. Encourage them to listen for:

The drumming of a woodpecker.
The buzzing of an insect.
Wind flowing through the trees.
The flow of water.
A bird calling.

Suggest these steps for creating a "Sound Map" on the paper or in their journal.

- Make a mark in the center of the page to indicate where you are sitting.
- For each sound you hear, draw a mark to indicate on the map how far away the sound is and the direction from which it is coming.
- Try to make marks that look like or are a color that represents the sound. The marks can be very simple: two wavy lines for the wind, a musical note for a bird, etc.
- Experiment with using your hands as "kangaroo ears" by cupping your hands behind your ears. Your cupped hands make a larger surface that reflects more sound into your ears. Then turn the cups backward and listen for sounds behind you.

Reconvene the group with some natural call — playing a flute, making an animal sound, etc. — for them to gather in a circle and share their experience and Sound Maps.

EXERCISE E: Three Changes
By Derek Harwell

This activity is designed to open the group's awareness of one another.

Materials: None

Time: 15 – 30 minutes

Space: 10 ft. X 20 ft. outdoors or indoors

Number of People: 2 – 30

Optimal Age: 10 and up

The Game:

- Have people pair off and stand opposite one another (forming two lines facing one another).
- Ask each person to look at the person across from them, encourage them to take in the whole person. (What are they wearing? What color are their eyes? Do they look tired? Energized? Happy?)
- After about a minute ask everyone to turn around such that the lines are facing away from one another.
- Ask each person to change three things about themselves.
- Have everyone turn around and have each person take turns with their partner guessing which three things the other has changed.

Debrief:

- What were some of the most dramatic and/or subtle changes?
- What made each change more or less dramatic/subtle?
- Why do we play this game?
    - observation skills
    - group awareness (as you are heading into the natural world are you watching out for one another — subtle changes in mood, attitude, awareness, etc.). This will help the group watch out for one another and learn from one another.

EXERCISE F: Camera

This activity is introduced as a way, through focusing, to become aware of how much is going on in an area, which upon first glance may not be that apparent.

Materials: A cloth bandana to serve as a blindfold for each participant.

Time: 30 minutes

Space: An area large enough for participants to walk around freely.

The Experience:
Invite the participants to select a partner. For the first 15 minutes, one of the pair will serve as the guide and the other as the one to be guided wearing the blindfold. The guide will lead their partner, carefully supporting them by their arm, to something to be focused on, i.e., a spider web, and after getting the person into location to view the web up close, the guide squeezes their partner's arm which is the clue for opening their eyes — taking a "snapshot" — and then squeezes the arm again to close their eyes and then be led to another thing to be focused upon. There is time for taking a snapshot of about four or five things and then the two change roles.

Afterwards participants are often surprised at how much is occurring in an area which may have seemed like "just a field."

EXERCISE G: Questions & BioQuiz To Direct Attention and Curiosity

GENERAL

1. Trace the water you drink from rainfall to tap. Where did the cloud gather its moisture? Trace its flow from your home to the ocean.

2. Choose a favorite meal and trace the ingredients back through the store... the processing plant...all the way to the soil. How many states (or countries?) participated? How many of the ingredients could you grow?

3. What kind of energy do you primarily use? Where does it come from? And at what cost to the environment?

4. When your garbage is thrown away, where is "away"?

5. What is recycled and where does it go?

6. List three critical environmental issues in your area. What can you do to help?

LOCAL

7. How many days until the moon is full?

8. Can you describe the soil around your home?

9. What is the average annual rainfall in your area?

10. When was the last time a fire burned in your area?

11. What were the primary subsistence techniques of the culture that lived in your area before you?

12. Name five edible plants in your region and the season in which they flower.

13. From what direction do winter storms generally come in your region?

14. Name five trees native to your region.

15. How long is the growing season where you live?

16. On what day of the year are the shadows the shortest where you live? The longest?

17. When do the deer rut in your region, and when are the young born?

18. Name five grasses in your area. Are any of them native?

19. Name five resident and five migratory birds in your area.

20. What primary ecological event/process influenced the landform where you live? What is the evidence?

21. What species have become extinct in your area?

22. Name five wild animals that live in your bioregion.

23. From where you're reading this, point north.

24. What spring wildflower is consistently among the first to bloom where you live?

25. Name five other wildflowers where you live.

26. Where is "wilderness" in your bioregion?

27. What are the major "natural" sounds you are aware of in any particular (name it) month or season?

28. What else are you curious about?

Information
Schedules & Flyers

Schedules

Close to Home
Oakland, California

Schedule of Saturday Field Trips
May 2006 – April 2007

May 13, 2006
Nature awareness day led by Paul Houghtaling of the Wilderness Awareness School. We'll be going to Briones Regional Park for exploration of nature through the lenses of sensory awareness training and bird language. All field trips include a 2-4 mile hike.

June 10
East Bay Regional Park Stewardship Manager Joe DiDonato will take us to Brushy Peak, a newly opened park in southern Alameda County, to learn about ground squirrels, considered the keystone species of the East Bay.

July 15
Naturalist Katie Colbert (EBRPD) will take us to Sunol Regional Wilderness to learn about the habitat and daily lives of rattlesnakes.

August 12
This will be a late afternoon/evening trip to Sunol Regional Wilderness led by naturalist Jessica Sheppard (resource analyst in the EBRPD Stewardship Dept.), where we will learn the importance of bats and their role in the ecosystem.

Sept 16
This is an excellent month to see dragonflies and learn about all their myriad shapes and dazzling colors. Our guide will be Kathy Biggs, a pioneer in popular dragonfly identification, at a private pond location near Orinda.

Oct 14
We'll carpool down to Don Edwards National Wildlife Refuge near San Jose to watch the antics of thousands of resident and migratory shorebirds. We'll focus on four species with our guide, Rusty Scalf, one of the Bay Area's best-known birding guides.

Nov 11
Doug Bell, Wildlife Manager for EBRPD, will introduce us to the prairie falcons that he is tracking for a district project. He will also contrast these raptors with the peregrine falcon.

Dec 9
Although we won't see one, we'll be looking for evidence of the mountain lions that inhabit the East Bay hills. We'll go with Rick Hopkins, wildlife biologist, who can teach us how to spot and identify lion paw prints and other signs. We'll learn how these large predators live undetected among us.

Jan 13, 2007
This is the month for newts, and they'll be swimming around in the labyrinths of Sibley Regional Park. Tom Tyler and Annie Prutzman, science educators, will take us on the hunt for these fascinating amphibians.

Feb 10
The creeks will be running, and this is an excellent time to see the rainbow trout that live in Redwood Canyon Park. Naturalist Pete Alexander (EBRPD fisheries program manager) will be our guide.

Mar 10
Ready for a truly charismatic species? Naturalist Mike Moran (EBRPD) will take us to see the tule elk that live on Grizzly Island in the Delta. Yes, there are elk in the East Bay.

April 14
We'll finish our yearlong program with a hike, a party and an evening visit to the truly exotic wildlife that live in the East Bay at the Oakland Zoo. This zoo has been recognized internationally for its work in habitat education and captive breeding programs. Close to Home will have a private evening led by a zoo naturalist. We're told the animals are much more lively at night.

Each Monday evening, prior to the field trip (June through March), we will have an expert speaker with slideshow presentation (or live animal) help us understand that month's species and how it fits into the ecosystem. These talks are also open to the public. They take place at Montclair Presbyterian Church Family Room in Oakland at 7:30 p.m. Joe DiDonato (EBRPD) will open our talk series on June 5 with a slideshow on ground squirrels.

Application available at Web site
www.close-to-home.org

Close to Home is a registered (nonprofit) organization in Alameda County.

Blue Ridge Sense of Place Program
North Carolina

ANNUAL SCHEDULE

September 6
Orientation

September 13 & 17
The Way It Was — The Old Growth Forest

October 11 & 15
The Cherokee — First People of the Blue Ridge

November 8 & 12
From the Ground Up — Our Rocks, Soils and Watershed

December 13 &17
Stargazing — Our Place Under the Sky

January 10 & 14
European Settlers — A Day in the Life of the Pioneers

February 14 & 18
Animals of the Blue Ridge — Who Was Here, Who Survived?

March 14 & 18
Asheville — The Paris of the South

April 11 & 15
Appalachian Spring

May 9 & 13
Farming and Wildcrafting in the Mountains of Western N.C.

June 13 & 17
Flora of the Highlands — Glaciation and Balds

July 11 & 15
The French Broad River

August 8 & 12
Climate of the Blue Ridge — What Might the Future Hold?

Discovering a Sense of Place

A yearlong journey through the Blue Ridge

This combined discussion and field study is offered
as a part of the *Blue Ridge Naturalist*,
an intergenerational program sponsored by
the North Carolina Center for Creative Retirement and
held in the Reuter Center on the UNC Asheville Campus.
The *Blue Ridge Naturalist* is funded
in part by a grant from the Western North Carolina
Community Foundation.

Tulip Tree

Ancient sunlight,
tall, true, and graceful
you grow
rooted Earth to Sky.

RICHARD FIREMAN
SENSE OF PLACE, NORTH CAROLINA

Cooper's Hawk, *Accipiter cooperii*

Baylands

Lone hawk hovering over
Restless waves of grass —
A sea of shoots yearning
in full sun.

JANA TUSCHMAN,
SENSE OF PLACE, PALO ALTO

Sense of Place Flyers & Ads

FEEL YOUR ROOTS GROW

Connect to yourself, the Earth and others.

Are you...

Yearning to connect to the natural world?

Wanting to experience your local watershed?

Eager to encounter the changing seasons?

Join us in a year-long in-depth exploration of our local region. One Monday evening and one Saturday per month from May 2006 - April 2007.

Exploring a Sense of Place

The Journey begins

Monday, May 8 at 7 p.m.

with a free Overview and Introduction

at

222 High Street, Palo Alto

For more details, visit us online at www.exploringsenseofplace.org, call 650.328.7756, or e-mail tom.cronin@sbcglobal.net.

Sample newspaper ad

E X P L O R I N G

A SENSE OF PLACE

FEEL YOUR ROOTS GROW

Connect to yourself, the Earth and others.

Are you...

Yearning for a sense of connection?

Wanting to spend more time with nature?

Interested in the natural wonders of this area?

Looking to meet interesting people?

Exploring a Sense of Place is a year-long, in-depth exploration of our local region with some of the area's most gifted naturalists. We meet one Monday evening and one Saturday per month from May 2006 - April 2007.

This program is designed to help you "come home" to your place in the natural world.

"You can't know who you are until you know where you are." Wendell Berry

Join us for a free Overview / Introduction on

Monday May 8, 2006. 7 - 9 pm at 222 High Street, Palo Alto

For more information (650) 328-7756 or

www.exploringsenseofplace.org

ORIGINATED AT THE FOUNDATION FOR GLOBAL COMMUNITY

A SENSE OF PLACE

EXPLORATIONS & SPEAKERS

Saturday adventures will meet to carpool or at the locations indicated and generally take place from 9:00 a.m. to 3:00 p.m.
Enrichment Evenings will be the previous Mondays from 7:00 to 9:00 p.m.

COST & REGISTRATION

The $375.00 registration fee covers the entire year-long program, including twelve Saturday Explorations, twelve Enrichment evenings, notebook materials, maps, docents, special guides and any entrance fees.
(Six-month registration available @ $200.00.)
For registration, visit www.fgconline.org/sense, or contact Tom Cronin or Karen Harwell at 650.328.7756 or e-mail us at senseofplace@fgconline.org .

DATE	THEME	LOCATION
Mon., May 8, 2006	Overview and Orientation	Fdn. for Global Community
Sat., May 27, 2006	Weather, Watershed, and Geology	Windy Hill
Sat., June 24, 2006	***Summer*** / The Oak Savannah	Foothill Park
Sat., July 22, 2006	Lower Watershed, and Riparian Environment	San Francisquito Creek
Sat., August 26, 2006	Solar System, Cosmology (Sunset Hike)	Russian Ridge Preserve
Sat., September 30, 2006	***Autumn*** / Food: Local, Seasonal and Organic	Hidden Villa
Sat., October 28, 2006	Life in an Estuary	Palo Alto Baylands
Sat., November 11, 2006	Upper Watershed, and Coastal Mountains	Huddart Park
Sat., December 9, 2006	***Winter*** / Creativity in Nature	Foothill Park
Sat., January 27, 2007	Wildlife Tracking and Ohlone Village	Jasper Ridge Preserve
Sat., February 24, 2007	Migrations and Reflections	Palo Alto Baylands
Sat., March 24, 2007	***Spring*** / Restoration & Preservation	Arastradero Preserve
Sat., April 28, 2007	Coming Home (Sunrise Celebration)	Windy Hill

Exploring a Sesnse of Place offers an opportunity for us to create new patterns in our lives by making ourselves available to new experiences, being imprinted by and becoming more intimate with the natural ecosystem in which we live. This course offers a chance to restore our connection with this particular place so that we can consciously choose how to participate in the world around us.

Sample flyer, front and back

Information
Resources

RESOURCES

Bioregionalism and Sense of Place

Alexander, Donald. "Bioregionalism: Science or Sensibility." *Environmental Ethics* v12: Summer 1990, pp. 161-174.

Andruss, Van et al. *Home! A Bioregional Reader*. New Society Pub: July 1990.

Hiss, Tony. *The Experience of Place*. Vintage Books: 1991.

Jackson, Wes. *Becoming Native to this Place*. Counterpoint Press: 1994.

Meyrowitz, Joshua. *No Sense of Place: The Impact of Electronic Media on Social Behavior.* Oxford University Press: 1985.

Murray, John A. *Bioregionalism in American Nature Writing*. Sierra Club Books: 1996.

Robertson, David. "Bioregionalism in American Nature Writing." In *American Nature Writing*. John A. Murray, editor. Sierra Club Books: 1996.

Sale, Kirkpatrick. *Dwellers in the Land: The Bioregional Vision*. Sierra Club: 1985.

Traina, Frank and Susan Darley-Hill, editors. *Perspectives in Bioregional Education.* North American Association for Environmental Education: 1995.

Welsh, Hartwell H., Jr. "Bioregions: An Ecological and Evolutionary Perspective and a Proposal for California." *California Fish and Game*, 80(3): Summer 1994, pp. 97-124.

Conservation, Preservation and Restoration

Berry, Wendell. *Home Economics: Fourteen Essays.* North Point Press: 1987.

Brower, David. *Let the Mountains Talk, Let the Rivers Run: A Call to Those Who Would Save the Earth.* New Society Publishers: 2000.

Bruges, James. *The Little Earth Book.* The Disinformation Company, Ltd.: 2000-2004.

Leopold, Aldo. *For the Health of the Land: Previously Unpublished Essays and Other Writings.* Island Press: 1999.

McPhee, John. *The Control of Nature.* Farrar Straus Giroux: 1989.

Mills, Stephanie. *In Service of the Wild: Restoring and Reinhabiting Damaged Land.* Beacon Press: 1995.

Roszak, Gomes, and Kanner, editors. *Ecopsychology: Restoring the Earth, Healing the Mind.* Sierra Club Books: 1995.

Silver, Cheryl Simon. *One Earth One Future: Our Changing Global Environment.* National Academy Press: 1990.

Steingraber, Sandra. *Living Downstream.* Vintage Books: 1998.

Culture and Place

Forbes, Peter. *The Great Remembering: Further Thoughts on Land, Soul, and Society.* The Trust for Public Land: 2001.

Griffin, Susan. *Woman and Nature: The Roaring Inside Her.* Sierra Club Books: 1978.

Nabhan, Gary Paul. *Cultures of Habitat: On Nature, Culture and Story.* Counterpoint: 1997.

Stewart and Gendar, editors. *Fools Paradise: A Carey McWilliams Reader.* Heyday Books: 2001.

Thomas, Lewis. *The Fragile Species.* Charles Scribner's Sons: 1992.

Designing with Nature

Ableman, Michael. *On Good Land: The Autobiography of an Urban Farm.* Chronicle Books: 1998.

Benyus, Janine. *Biomimicry: Innovation Inspired by Nature.* William Morrow and Company, Inc.: 1997.

Kellert, Stephen R. and Edward O. Wilson, editors. *The Biophilia Hypothesis.* Island Press: 1993.

Shepard, Paul, editor. *The Only World We've Got: A Paul Shepard Reader.* Sierra Club Books: 1996.

Vitek, William and Wes Jackson, editors. *Rooted in the Land: Essays on Community and Place.* Yale University Press: 1996.

Wilson, Edward O. *In Search of Nature.* Island Press: 1996.

Ecology

Bortoft, Henri. *The Wholeness of Nature.* Lindisfarne Books: 1996.

Bruchac, Joseph and Michael Caduto. *Keepers of the Earth.* Golden, Colorado. Fulcrum Publishing: 1989.

Callenbach, Ernest. *Ecology*. University of California Press: 1998.

Daily, Gretchen, editor. *Nature's Services: Societal Dependence on Natural Ecosystems.* Island Press: 1997.

Eldredge, Niles. *Life on the Balance: Humanity and the Biodiversity Crisis.* Princeton University Press: 1998.

Gore, Al. *Earth in the Balance: Ecology and the Human Spirit.* Houghton Mifflin: 1992.

Hayden, Tom. *The Lost Gospel of the Earth.* Merlin Publishing: September 1996.

Marshall, Peter. *Nature's Web: Rethinking Our Place on Earth.* M.E. Sharpe, Inc.: 1996.

Orr, David. *Earth in Mind: On Education, Environment, and the Human Prospect.* Island Press: 1994.

Pimm, Stuart L. *A Scientist Audits the Earth.* Rutgers University Press: 2001.

Tucker, Mary Evelyn and John A. Grim, editors. *Worldviews and Ecology: Religion, Philosophy, and the Environment.* Orbis Books: 1994.

Uhl, Christopher. *Developing Ecological Consciousness: Path to a Sustainable World.* Rowman & Littlefield Publishers, Inc.: 2004.

Wilson, Edward O. *The Future of Life.* Alfred A. Knopf: 2002.

Earth Literacy

Crabtree, Margo, editor. *Ecoliteracy: Mapping the Terrain.* Center For Ecoliteracy: 2000.

Elder, John. *Stories in the Land: A Place-Based Environmental Education Anthology.* Nature Literacy Series, Number 2, The Orion Society: 1998.

Smith, McGregor, Jr. *Now That You Know: A Journey Toward Earth Literacy.* Earth Knows Publications: 1997.

Van Matre, Steve. *Earth Education: A New Beginning.* The Institute for Earth Education Cedar Cove: 1990.

Nature Anthologies

Barnhill, David Landis, editor. *At Home on the Earth: Becoming Native to Our Place.* University of California Press: 1999.

Forbes, Forbes and Whybrow, editors. *Our Land, Ourselves: Readings on People and Place.* The Trust for Public Land, San Francisco: 1999.

Gardner, Jason, editor. *The Sacred Earth: Writers on Nature and Spirit.* New World Library: 1998.

Halpern, Daniel, editor. *On Nature: Nature, Landscape, and Natural History.* North Point Press: 1987.

Jensen, Derrick, editor. *Listening to the Land: Conversations about Nature, Culture, and Eros.* Sierra Club Press: 1995.

Van Matre, Steve and Bill Weiler, editors. *The Earth Speaks.* The Institute for Earth Education: 1983.

Willers, Bill, editor. *Learning to Listen to the Land.* Island Press: 1991.

Nature Essays

Ackerman, Diane. *A Natural History of the Senses.* Harper Collins: 1991.

Berry, Wendell. *The Art of the Common Place: The Agrarian Essays of Wendell Berry.* Counterpoint: 2002.

Cornell, Joseph. *John Muir: My Life with Nature.* Dawn Publications: 2000.

Daniel, John. *The Trail Home: Nature, Imagination, and the American West.* Pantheon Books: 1994.

Dillard, Annie. *Pilgrim at Tinker Creek.* Harper Perennial: 1974.

Duncan, David James. *My Story as Told by Water.* Sierra Club Books: 2001.

Eiseley, Loren. *The Immense Journey.* Time-Life Books: 1962.

Elder, John. *Imagining the Earth: Poetry and the Vision of Nature.* University of Illinois Press: 1985.

Savage, Candace. *Curious by Nature: One Woman's Exploration of the Natural World.* Grey Stone Books: 2005.

Snyder, Gary. *A Place in Space: Ethics, Aesthetics and Watersheds.* Counterpoint: 1995.

Snyder, Gary. *The Practice of the Wild.* North Point Press: 1990.

Stegner, Wallace. *Where the Bluebird Sings to the Lemonade Springs.* Penguin: 1992.

Swain, Roger. *Earthly Pleasures: Tales from a Biologist's Garden.* Charles Scribner's Sons: 1981.

Van der Post, Laurens. *A Far-Off Place.* Harcourt Brace: 1974.

Williams, Terry Tempest. *An Unspoken Hunger: Stories from the Field.* Pantheon Books: 1994.

California Nature Writings

Beers, Terry, editor. *Unfolding Beauty: Celebrating California's Landscapes.* Heyday Books: 2000.

Buckley, Christopher and Gary Young, editors. *The Geography of Home: California's Poetry of Place.* Heyday Books: 1999.

Didion, Joan. *Where I Was From.* Alfred A. Knopf: 2003.

Gilbar, Steven. *Natural State: A Literary Anthology of California Nature Writing.* University of California Press: 1998.

Haslam, Gerald, editor. *Jack London's Golden State: Selected California Writings.* Heyday Books: 1999.

Merchant, Carolyn, editor. *Green Versus Gold: Sources in California's Environmental History.* Island Press: 1998.

Paddison, Joshua, editor. *A World Transformed: Firsthand Accounts of California Before the Gold Rush.* Heyday Books: 1999.

Van der Veer, Judy. *November Grass: A Novel.* Heyday Books: 2001.

Our Place in the Cosmos

Raymo, Chet. *The Path: A One-Mile Walk Through the Universe.* Walker & Co.: 2003.

Swimme, Brian and Thomas Berry. *The Universe Story: From the Primordial Flaring Forth to the Ecozoic Era, A Celebration of the Unfolding of the Cosmos.* Harper Collins: 1992.

FIELD GUIDES

There are several excellent field guide series to help you identify birds, plants, animals, insects and even stars. You can find guides specific to the wildlife in your area.

Wildlife Guides

American Bird Conservancy Field Guides (Harper Perennial)
Guides on specific types of birds, including birds of North America, water birds, backyard birds, birds of prey, etc.

American Bird Conservancy Compact Guides (Harper Perennial)
Guides on birds that can be observed at specific sites.

National Audubon Society Nature Guides (Alfred A. Knopf)
Guides for Western Forests, Atlantic and Gulf Coasts, Deserts, Eastern Forests, Grasslands, Pacific Coast and Wetlands.

Peterson Field Guides
(Houghton Mifflin)
45 guides on topics ranging from eastern birds to western forests.

Peterson First Guides
(Houghton Mifflin)
Condensed versions of the Peterson Field Guides, focused on the animals, plants and other natural things you are most likely to see.

Princeton Field Guides
(Princeton University Press)
Many fine guides, including *Mammals of North America,* and guides on plants and animals on other continents.

California Guides

Alden, Peter and Fred Heath. *National Audubon Society Field Guide to California.* Alfred A. Knopf: 1998.

Bakker, Elna. *An Island Called California: An Ecological Introduction to Its Natural Communities.* University of California Press: 1984.

Brown, Ann Marie. *Foghorn Outdoors 101 Great Hikes of the San Francisco Bay Area,* 2nd ed. Avalon Travel Publishing: 2003.

Conradson, Diane R. *Exploring Our Baylands.* San Francisco Bay Wildlife Society: 1996.

Crowder, Spangle and Rusmore. *Peninsula Trails: Outdoor Adventures on the San Francisco Peninsula.* 3rd ed. Wilderness Press: 1997.

Doss, Margoot Patterson. *A Walker's Yearbook: 52 Seasonal Walks in the San Francisco Bay Area.* Presidio Press: 1983.

Gustaitis, Rasa, editor. *San Francisco Bay Shoreline Guide: A California State Coastal Conservancy Book.* University of California Press: 1995.

McMillon, Bill. *Seasonal Guide to the Natural Year.* Fulcrum Publishing: 1995.

Peeters, Hans and Pam Peeters. *Raptors of California: A California Natural History Guide.* University of California Press: 2005. (See also other guides in this series.)

Rowell, Galen A. *Bay Area Wild: A Celebration of the Natural Heritage of the San Francisco Bay Area.* Sierra Club Books: 1997.

Rusmore, Jean, Frances Spangle and Betsy Crowder. *Peninsula Trails: Outdoor Adventures on the San Francisco Peninsula.* Wilderness Press: 1997.

Soares, John and Marc Soares. *100 Hikes in Northern California.* The Mountaineers: 1994.

Weintraub, David. *Peninsula Tales and Trails: Commemorating the 13th Anniversary of the Midpeninsula Regional Open Space District.* Westwind Press: 2004.

West, Don and Joseph Cotchett. *The Coast Time Forgot: The Complete Tour Guide to the San Mateo Coast.* Thornton House: 2002.

RESOURCES FOR NATURE AWARENESS EXERCISES

Abram, David. *The Spell of the Sensuous: Perception and Language in a More than Human World.* Vintage Books: 1997.

Joseph Cornell. *Listening to Nature: How to Deepen Your Awareness of Nature.* Dawn Publications: 1987.

Joseph Cornell. *Sharing Nature with Children.* Dawn Publications: 1998.

Joseph Cornell. *Sharing Nature with Children II.* Dawn Publications: 1989.

Joseph Cornell. *Sharing the Joy of Nature: Nature Activities for All Ages.* Dawn Publications: 1998.

Joseph Cornell. *With Beauty Before Me: An Inspirational Guide for Nature Walks.* Dawn Publications: 2000.

Cook, Charles. *Awakening to Nature: Renewing Your Life by Connecting with the Natural World.* McGraw-Hill/Contemporary Books: 2001.

Cornell, Joseph and Michael Deranja. *Journey to the Heart of Nature: A Guided Exploration.* Dawn Publications: 1994.

Devereux, Paul. *Re-Visioning the Earth: A Guide to Opening the Healing Channels between Minds and Nature.* Fireside: 1996.

Endredy, James and Victor Sanchez. *Earthwalks for Body and Spirit: Exercises to Restore Our Sacred Bond with the Earth.* Inner Traditions Intl Ltd.: 2002.

Henley, Thom. *Rediscovery: Ancient Pathways – New Directions, A Guidebook to Outdoor Education.* Western Canada Wilderness Committee: 1989.

Jacobs, Warren David and Karen I. Shragg, editors. *Tree Stories: A Collection of Extraordinary Encounters.* SunStripe Press Publications.

FINDING THE STORIES OF YOUR PLACE

Deep-Time Geologic Story

Alt, David D. and Donald W. Hyndman. *Roadside Geology of Northern California.* Mountain Press Publishing Company: 1981.

Apt, Jay, Michael Helfert and Justin Wilkinson. *Orbit: NASA Astronauts Photograph the Earth.* Roger Ressmeyer, editor. National Geographic Society: 1996.

Cornelius, Geoffrey and Paul Devereux. *The Secret Language of the Stars and Planets: A Visual Key to the Heavens.* Duncan Baird Publishers: 1996.

Fortey, Richard. *Earth: An Intimate History.* Alfred A. Knopf: 2004.

Gribbin, John and Simon Goodwin. *Origins: Our Place in Hubble's Universe.* The Overlook Press, Peter Mayer Publishers, Inc.: 1998.

Hatchett, Clint and Stephen Marchesi, illustrator. *The Glow-in-the-Dark Night Sky Book.* Random House, Inc.: 1988.

Howard, Arthur D. *Geologic History of Middle California.* University of California Press: 1979.

The Hubble Telescope – 2001 Calendar. The Ink Group (www.inkgroup.com).

Liebes, Sahtouris and Swimme. *A Walk Through Time: From Stardust to Us – The Evolution of Life on Earth.* John Wiley & Sons: 1998.

Ridpath, Ian. *Stars and Planets.* DK Smithsonian Handbooks, Dorling Kindersley Limited: 2002.

Ronan, Colin A. *The Natural History of the Universe: From the Big Bang to the End of Time.* MacMillan Publishing Co.: 1991.

Stevens, Payson R. and Kevin W. Kelley. *Embracing Earth: New Views of Our Changing Planet.* Chronicle Books: 1992.

Trefil, James. *Other Worlds: Images of the Cosmos from Earth and Space.* National Geographic Society: 1999.

Weather and Climate

Day , John A. and Vincent J. Schaefer. *Peterson First Guides to Clouds and Weather: A Simplified Field Guide to the Atmosphere.* Pocket edition. Houghton Mifflin Company: 1998.

Ellyard, David, consulting editor. *Weather.* The Nature Company Discoveries Library, Time Life Books: 1996.

Gilliam, Harold. *Weather of the San Francisco Bay Region.* University of California Press: 1962.

Stewart, George R. *Storm.* Heyday Books: 1941.

Indigenous Peoples' Ways

Blackburn and Anderson, editors. *Before the Wilderness: Environmental Management by Native Californians.* Ballena Press: 1993.

Heizer, Robert F. and Albert B. Elsasser. *The Natural World of the California Indians.* University of California Press: 1980.

Knudtson, Peter and David Suzuki. *Wisdom of the Elders: Sacred Native Stories of Nature.* Reprint edition. Bantam: 1993.

Margolin, Malcolm. *The Ohlone Way: Indian Life in the San Francisco-Monterey Bay Area.* Heyday Books: 1978.

Versluis, Arthur. *Sacred Earth: The Spiritual Landscape of Native America.* Inner Traditions International: 1992.

Wildlife

Kavanagh, James. *The Nature of California: An Introduction to Familiar Plants and Animals and Natural Attractions.* Waterford Field Guides: 1997.

Margolin, Malcolm. *The Earth Manual: How to Work on Wild Land Without Taming It.* Heyday Books: 1985.

Quinn, John R. *Wildlife Survivors: The Flora and Fauna of Tomorrow.* McGraw-Hill: 1994.

Plants

Carolin, Roger, consulting editor. *Incredible Plants.* The Nature Company Discoveries Library, Time-Life Books: 1997.

Ferris, Roxana S. *Native Shrubs of the San Francisco Bay Region.* University of California Press: 1968.

Heinrich, Bernd. *The Trees in My Forest.* Cliff Street Books: 1997.

Johnstone, Peter, editor. *Giants in the Earth: The California Redwoods.* Heyday Books: 2001.

Kozoloff , Eugene N. and Linda H. Beidleman. *Plants of the San Francisco Bay Region; Mendocino to Monterey.* Sagen Press: 1994.

Lyons, Cooney-Lazaneo and King. *Plants of the Coast Redwood Region.* The Looking Press: 1988.

Pollan, Michael. *The Botany of Desire: A Plant's Eye View of the World.* Random House: 2002.

Roos-Collins, Margit. *The Flavors of Home: A Guide to Wild Edible Plants of the San Francisco Bay Area.* Heyday Books: 1990.

Schmidt, Marjorie G. *Growing California Native Plants.* University of California Press: 1980.

Animals

Boone, J. Allen. *Kinship With All Life.* Harper & Row, Publishers, Inc.: 1954.

Clark, Jeanne. *California Wildlife Viewing Guide.* Falcon Publishing: 1996.

Landau, Diana, Shelley Stump and The California Center for Wildlife. *Living with Wildlife: How to Enjoy, Cope with, and Protect North America's Wild Creatures Around Your Home and Theirs.* Sierra Club Books: 1994.

Rezendes, Paul. *Tracking and the Art of Seeing: How to Read Animal Tracks and Signs.* 2nd edition. Harper Collins: 1999.

Rezendes, Paul. *The Wild Within: Adventures in Nature and Animal Tracking.* Penguin Putnam Inc.: 1998.

Stokes, Donald and Lillian Stokes. *Animal Tracking and Behavior.* Little, Brown & Company: 1986.

Birds

Elphick, Dunning, and Sibley, editors. *The Sibley Guide to Bird Life & Behavior.* National Audubon Society, Alfred A. Knopf: 2001.

Fisher, Chris and Joseph Morlan. *Birds of San Francisco and the Bay Area.* Lone Pine Publishing: 1996.

Habegger and Carlson, editors. *The Gift of Birds: True Encounters with Avian Spirits.* Travelers' Tales, Inc.: 1999.

Hill, Jen, editor. *An Exhilaration of Wings: The Literature of Birdwatching.* Penguin Books: 1999.

Pelikan, Judy. *The Music of Wild Birds: An Illustrated, Annotated, and Opinionated Guide to Fifty Birds and Their Songs.* Algonquin Books of Chapel Hill: 2004.

Rothenberg, David. *Why Birds Sing: A Journey into the Mystery of Bird Song.* Basic Books: 2005.

Insects

Lauck, Joanne Elizabeth. *The Voice of the Infinite in the Small: Revisioning the Insect-Human Connection.* Swan, Raven & Co.: 1998.

STORY OF LIFE

Capra, Fritjof. *The Web of Life: A New Scientific Understanding of Living Systems.* Anchor Books: 1996.

Earle, Sylvia A. *Sea Change: A Message of the Oceans.* Ballantine Books: 1995.

Fortey, Richard. *Life: A Natural History of the First Four Billion Years of Life on Earth.* Alfred A. Knopf: 1997.

Lovelock, James. *Gaia: A New Look at Life on Earth.* Oxford University Press: 1995.

Margulis, Lynn and Dorion Sagan. *What Is Life?* Simon & Schuster: 1995.

SPIRIT AND NATURE

Barlow, Connie. *Green Space, Green Time: The Way of Science.* Springer-Verlag: 1997.

Berry, Thomas. *Dream of the Earth.* Sierra Club Publisher: 1990.

Berry, Thomas. *The Great Work: Our Way into the Future.* Bell Tower: 1999.

Goodenough, Ursula. *The Sacred Depths of Nature.* Oxford University Press: 1998.

Ray, Veronica. *Green Spirituality: Reflections on Belonging to a World Beyond Myself.* Hazelden Books: 1992.

Rockefeller, Steven and John Elder, editors. *Spirit and Nature: Why the Environment Is a Religious Issue.* Beacon Press: 1992.

Swan, James A. *Sacred Places: How the Living Earth Seeks Our Friendship.* Bear & Co. Inc.: 1990.

Suzuki, David. *The Sacred Balance: Rediscovering our Place in Nature.* 2nd revised edition. Mountaineers Books: 2002. (Also look for the PBS series on DVD with the same name.)

Teilhard de Chardin. *Building the Earth.* Dimension Books, Inc.: 1965.

WEB SITES

(There are many informative Web sites. Here are a few to get you started.)

Acterra
www.acterra.org

Bay Area Open Space Council
www.bayareaopenspacecouncil.org

Bay Area Trail
www.abag.ca.gov/bayareatrail/baytrail.html

Bay Nature Magazine
www.baynature.com

Blue Ridge Naturalist &
Sense of Place Program
www.unca.edu/ncccr/brnp

California Native Plant Society
www.cnps.org

Close to Home – Exploring Nature's Treasures in the East Bay
www.close-to-home.org

Committee for Green Foothills
www.greenfoothills.org

East Bay Regional Park District
www.ebparks.org

Great River Earth Institute (bioregionalism)
www.greatriv.org/bioreg.htm#bioreg

Greenbelt Alliance
www.greenbelt.org

Hidden Villa
www.hiddenvilla.org

Hooked on Nature (connecting children with nature)
www.hookedonnature.org

Marine Mammal Center
www.marinemammalcenter.org

Midpeninsula Regional Open Space District
www.openspace.org

The Night Sky Planisphere (to order)
www.astromax.com/chandler/nightsky.htm

Northwest Earth Institute (discussion courses, including bioregionalism, deep ecology, sense of place)
www.nwei.org

Peninsula Open Space Trust
www.openspacetrust.org

San Francisco Bay Area Open Space
www.openspace.org

San Francisco Bay Ecology:
Marine Science Institute
www.sfbaymsi.org/ecology.htm

Save the Bay
www.savesfbay.org

Sierra Club
www.sierraclub.org

U.S. Geological Survey
www.sfbay.wr.usgs.gov
www.usgs.gov

Waste-Free Lunches (how to pack a waste-free lunch.)
www.wastefreelunches.org

World Watch Institute
www.worldwatch.org

VIDEOS & DVD's

Blue Planet. Smithsonian Institution/Lockheed Corporation.

A Sense of Place: What Is the Appropriate Relationshhip Between Humans and the Whole Living System? Interviews with Kirkpatrick Sale, John and Nancy Jack Todd, Paul Winter and Jeff Bercuvitz. A Baylands Production: 1994.
(To order this and other excellent videos, go to: www.hookedonnature.org)

Wild California: A Musical Journey Into the Natural Beauty of California's Wilderness. Sea Studios: 1989.

Eyewitness Videos

Pond & River. Martin Sheen, narrator. DK Vision: 1996 (www.dk.com).

Weather. Martin Sheen, narrator.
DK Vision: 1996 (www.dk.com).

Production Credits

Editorial

Ariel Rubissow Okamoto
Kathleen Wong
(participant interviews)
Kathryn Ankrum (copyediting)

Design

Darren Campeau
www.dcampeau.com

Photography

Sam Bloomberg-Rissman, Dave Sanger Photography
p. 19

Maggie Hallahan Photography
www.maggiehallahan.com
(415) 441-5300
pp. 2, 4, 10, 11 (left), 14, 15 (upper), 18, 29 (left), 32, 34, 36, 40, 41, 45, 47, 50 (upper), 51

Sidney J.P. Hollister
465 Chestnut St., SF, CA 94133
(415) 772-8903
pp. 5, 8, 15, 16, 19, 25, 29, 31, 33, 37, 42, 55

QT Luong
Cover landscape photo

Bryce Perry
p. 13

Stu Selland
pp. 11 (right), 20, 24, 30, 53

Sense of Place Participants
pp. 6, 9, 12 (both), 27, 28, 39, 43, 44, 48, 49, 50 (lower), 52

Jerry Ulrey (Blue Ridge) p. 35

Illustrations

Special thanks to the University of California Press for permission to use illustrations from the following books:

Dragonflies and Damselflies of California
Written and illustrated by Tim Manolis.
California Natural History Guides No. 72,
UC Press, 2003.
Larva p. 10 (p.19); Blue-eyed darner p. 28 (PL 16).

Mammals of California
By E.W. Jameson, Jr., Illustrations by Hans J. Peters.
California Natural History Guides No. 66, UC Press, 2004.
Coyote and gray wolf p. 13 (Fig. 4, p. 169); Raccoon and opossum tracks p. 15 (Fig. 2, p. 8); California meadow vole p. 26 (Fig. 131, p. 346); Mule deer p. 28 (Fig. 89, p. 246); Wood rat p. 32 (Fig. 123, p. 327); Striped skunk p. 33 (fig. 48, p. 185); Black-tailed jackrabbit p. 40 (Fig. 141, p. 362).

Early Uses of California Plants
By Edward K. Balls, Illustrations by
Stephen Tillett & Richard Beasley.
California Natural History Guide,
UC Press, 1962.
Mesquite p. 11 (p. 20); Prickly-pear p. 28 (p. 37); Seablite p. 31 (p. 81); Barrel cactus p. 45 (p. 43).

Plants of the San Francisco Bay Region, Mendocino to Monterey
By Linda H. Beidleman & Eugene N. Kozloff,
Illustrations by Jeanne R. Janish.
UC Press, 2003.
Western labrador tea p. 6 (p. 197); California pine-foot p. 7 (p. 197); Western sycamore p. 12 (p. 277); Carpetweed p. 26 (p. 257); California burclover p. 29 (p. 207); Tanbark oak p. 30 (p. 223); Western peony p. 30 (p. 272); Salt rush p. 31 (p. 377); Wild celery p. 32 (p. 87); Douglas microseris and Spanish thistle p. 43 (p. 103); Cheat grass p. 44 (p.405); Great water speedwell p. 51 & 81 (p. 331); Coltsfoot p. 52 (p. 103); Mat sandbur p. 53 (p. 405); Germander speedwell p. 63 (p. 331); Whitevien shinleaf p. 67 (p. 197); Coltsfoot p. 75 (p. 103); Torrent sedge p. 85 (p. 359).

Trees and Shrubs of California
By John D. Stuart & John O. Sawyer,
Illustrations by Andrea J. Pickart.
California Natural History Guide No. 62,
UC Press, 2001.
Calif. blackberry p. 17 (Fig 185, p. 367); Tanoak p. 22 (Fig. 128, p. 267); Mock azalea p. 27 (Fig. 134, p. 276); Western azalea p. 27 (Fig. 173, p. 342); Blue oak p. 34 (Fig. 160, p. 321); Black willow p. 34 (Fig. 187, p. 372); Velvet ash p. 36 (Fig. 111,p. 241); Scotch broom p. 37 (Fig. 101, p. 225); Red osier p. 38 (Fig 98, p. 220); Gorse p. 39 (Fig. 200, p. 402); Wild mock-orange p. 39 (Fig. 140, p. 285); Hop sage p. 40 (Fig. 116, p. 248); Choke cherry p. 40 (Fig. 153, p. 308); Bladderpod p. 41 (Fig. 120, p. 254); Silver buffaloberry p. 42 (Fig. 192, p. 388).

Shore Wildflowers of California, Oregon and Washington
By Philip A. Munz, Illustrations by Jeanne Janish.
UC Press, 1964.
Brake p. 9, Barberry p. 18, (Fig. 5, p.10); Casacara p. 9 (Fig. 144, p. 98); Coast live oak p. 13 (Fig. 175, p. 111); Monterey pine p. 17 (Fig. 163, p. 107); Miner's lettuce p. 35 (Fig, 124, p. 92).

Other Illustrations

Elise Hillend
Presidio clarksia p. 35

Note:

Two illustrations came from unknown original sources: killdeer p. 14, clapper rail p. 49.